# Fish Cookery

**OUTDOOR LIFE TAKE-ALONG BOOKS**

# Fish Cookery

## Mel Marshall

*Drawings by Tom Beecham*

**OUTDOOR LIFE • HARPER & ROW**

**NEW YORK    LONDON**

# CONTENTS

# INTRODUCTION

Fortunate is the angler who cooks his own catch, for he will enjoy fish at its finest.

This little saying, like so many generalities, is basically true, but it has a few strings tied to it. There are conditions attached, a few "ifs" that must be observed.

It's true *if* the fisherman-turned-cook gives the fish he catches the proper care. Principally, this means cleaning the fish you intend to keep and cook immediately after you land them, or seeing to it that your keepers stay alive until they can be cleaned.

It's true *if* the cook understands the one big difference between cooking fish and other foods. The objective in cooking most foods is to make them tender, while fish should be cooked only long enough to coagulate their body juices and set their flesh. Overcooking fish destroys both their tenderness and their flavor.

It's true *if* the cook equips himself properly; some kitchen utensils are completely unsuited to the job of cooking fish.

Finally, it's true *if* the cook uses a light and discriminating, yet adventuresome hand in seasoning. This is not as contradictory as it might appear at first glance, as recipes in this book will demonstrate.

None of these "ifs" is difficult to observe. All are important, if as the axiom above promises, you want to enjoy fish at its finest. Cooking your

1

catch should be part of the pleasure you get from fishing. A few favorite recipes are as important to your angling enjoyment as your favorite rod, flies, and lures. And enjoyment is what this book is about.

# 1

## CLEANING AND FILLETING

Like just about any other job you might name, *if* you know how to do it, cleaning a fish is both easy and quick. Any fish suitable for eating can be cleaned in less than one minute—with practice, in something like half that time—and without getting your hands smeared up to the elbows.

Surprisingly, a lot of anglers who are experts at luring and landing fish have never learned how to clean them. They make a messy, agonizing job out of what should be a simple, fast operation. Some of these fellows who shy away from cleaning fish have found the easiest way of all to do the job; they turn it over to their wives. This is fine, up to a point, but it's a pretty good bet that fishing and fishermen would be a lot more popular with wives if the ladies didn't find themselves stuck with the job of cleaning as well as cooking what their angling husbands bring home.

Besides the fact that streamside cleaning relieves the strain on family ties created by passing your catch along to your wife to prepare, there is a sound, practical reason why cleaning fish immediately after taking them from the water should become a habit with every fisherman.

Because fish never really stop feeding, nature has given them an amazingly efficient apparatus for digesting their food. Once, while fishing the glass-clear waters of Yosemite National Park, I climbed out to the bank to detour around a hole too deep to wade. The bank was high, six or eight feet above the water's surface, and each grain of sand on the stream's bottom was clearly visible. I was walking slowly and quietly, studying the water, when I saw what was an obvious biological impossibility: a trout with a tail at each end of its body, hanging motionless in the current.

It took a few minutes of study to deduce that I was looking at a brown trout of four or five pounds that had gulped down and was in the process of swallowing another trout weighing perhaps half that much. The tail of the trout being eaten stuck out of the bigger fish's mouth a good six or seven inches, which explained the illusion of the double-tailed trout.

This was something too fascinating to ignore. I laid my rod aside and sat down to watch. Darkness shaded the water before the smaller fish was completely consumed, but in the two hours that I observed the process, the big trout ingested between four and five inches of its victim's body, at a rate of roughly an inch per half-hour.

Unlike many fish stories, this one has a moral: the gastric juices of a fish work very quickly indeed. Nor does the digestive process stop after a fish dies. A living fish has stomach secretions that prevent its gastric juices from digesting its stomach walls. But these delicate secretions lose their effectiveness immediately, while the gastric juices keep working after death. In a very short time they will eat away the stomach walls and taint the flesh. The actual time required varies with the quantity of undigested matter in its stomach when death occurs and the air temperature. Given an empty stomach and a warm, humid day, the process may occur in as short a time as a half-hour. So, clean your fish immediately after they are taken to avoid the foul taste these digestive juices will give a fish's flesh.

Ideally, fish should be kept alive until the last possible moment before they are to be cleaned for cooking. If you are wading deep water and wearing a willow creel that is submerged most of the time, there is no problem. In shallow water, or when fishing from the bank or a boat, use a metal mesh fish basket with a long stout cord tied to its handle; the fish will survive during the brief periods you lift the basket from the water while moving to another spot. A live-well in a boat is not just ornamental; if used, it keeps your fish alive. Yet, many anglers toss their catch on the boat's floorboards to die, dry, and spoil in the sunshine.

A snap stringer will keep fish alive if the holding hooks are put through both lips. A cord stringer that is passed through mouth and gilly usually results in dead fish. Unventilated creels of treated cloth or plastic not only kill fish put into them, but speed spoilage by snuggling to your warm body. The gunny sack of the bank-fishing small boy usually suffocates the fish it contains even if the sack is submerged. And the angler who tosses his fish into a bucket of water, hoping they will stay in good condition until he gets around to cleaning them several hours later, is hoping in vain.

Damage from gastric secretions is only part of the reason to kill and clean your fish the moment they come from the water, or keep them alive until you are ready to clean them. While alive, fish have a delicate coating of mucus covering their entire body; after death, this coating hardens quickly and becomes difficult to remove. If a dead fish is wetted, this mucus turns into slime; this is why a wet dead fish is so slippery and hard to hold. If the fish is taken from the water, killed at once, and cleaned within a few minutes without being washed first, the mucus coating can easily be wiped off and the fish will not be hard to handle.

## Keeping Fish Cool

If you do not have facilities for keeping fish alive until the moment of cleaning, then clean them at once and keep the cleaned fish cool. There are several ways to do this. The old willow creel with a few ferns or leaves from streamside bushes tossed loosely into its bottom has yet to be equalled for temporary storage of cleaned fish. In areas where flies, wasps, and yellowjackets are not bothersome, simply hanging the fish by the jaw in the shade of a tree, on a twig, will keep them in better condition than if you wrap them tightly in paper or foil. Where it is hot and humid, fish should not be hung this way, of course, and even in the cool dry air of high altitudes they should not be allowed to hang for more than a few hours.

In days before portable ice chests were a standard item of fishermen's equipment, I did a great deal of trout fishing at altitudes of 7,000 feet and above. Fish taken the last morning of the trip were washed in the icy water after being cleaned, hung up to drip for a few minutes, then rolled up in the middle of a sleeping bag for packing out. They would be in good shape, still cold to the touch, a half-day later when unpacked at home. This trick still works, if you are in the proper surroundings and have no other means to keep fish cool when taking them home from camp.

Portable ice chests, of course, are fine. The foam plastic type can be used with ice or with the reusable pouches and cans of liquid that are frozen at home—the latter are in many ways more convenient than ice. Foam plastic ice chests are generally not practical if dry ice is the refrigerant; its extreme cold will cause the plastic to crack, and all these plastic containers allow so much air inside that dry ice vanishes quickly. Metal ice chests are needed if dry ice is going to be used, and you should not handle dry ice with bare hands. Be sure the dealer from whom you buy it wraps it in the special paper he keeps on hand for this purpose.

In many high mountain areas you will find snowbanks in sheltered places through most of the summer, and your cleaned fish can be slipped into the snow for preservation. When fishing through the ice in winter on the lakes of the upper Midwest, you certainly have no problems; just toss your fish outside the shanty and let nature take over.

This brings up the question of freezing fish to preserve them. It can be done, and with little loss of quality or flavor. The secret is to freeze the entire fish into a block of ice, which prevents both loss of moisture and freezer-burn during storage. Small fish, measuring less than ten inches after their heads and tails have been removed in cleaning, can be frozen in a regular ice tray in a home refrigerator. Prepare the tray by freezing a thin film of ice (no more than ¼ inch thick) in its bottom, before putting in the fish. Then, cover the fish completely with very cold water and freeze at once.

Bigger fish can be frozen this way in trays made of heavy aluminum foil. If there is a commercial freezing plant with a cooperative operator reasonably close to your fishing area, you can bring home all the fish the law permits by using this technique. It's better than wrapping the fish in foil, film, or freezer-paper, though it does result in a bulky, heavy bundle. When cooking fish that have been frozen in this fashion, their icy jacket should be melted quickly under running water and the fish cooked at once.

## Easy-Cleaning Technique

Now, at long last, we're coming to that easy cleaning technique hinted at in the opening lines of this chapter. Once you've mastered the few simple cuts necessary, you'll wonder why you ever thought that cleaning a fish was an onerous chore. This method works with all but one or two species of fish—such as catfish, which must be skinned. And if any species dealt with in the recipes that follow require special attention in cleaning or preparation, the fact will be noted along with the recipe.

**Start cleaning your fish** at the head, not the vent. The tongue, gullet, gills, and intestinal cluster of a fish are a single, interconnected unit and can be more easily detached from the front than from the rear. Open the fish's mouth wide, and with the tip of a very sharp knife cut the narrow strip of gristle at the top and back of the mouth, which joins the gills to the head. On the body of the fish, right in back of the gill plates, there is a bony ridge, and then a thin membrane. Run the tip of your knife through the membrane, between the ridge and the fish's body, and cut from the top of the body to the tip of the lower jaw. Do this on both sides.

At the tip of the jaw, a strip of gristle connects bone and tongue; cut through this gristle. Now, run the tip of your knife from the jaw in back of the gill line along the fish's belly to the anal orifice; make this cut shallow, just deep enough to part the skin and thin layer of belly flesh. This is the only really tricky cut. It must be deep enough to open the cavity, but not so deep that it will puncture stomach or intestines. On my fish-cleaning knives, I grind a wide V between ⅛ inch and ¼ inch from the tip and sharpen this V to a razor edge with a fishhook honing stone. The V gives you almost automatically the correct depth for the belly cut.

Hook your finger through the bottom of the gill cut, around the fish's tongue, and give one quick, sharp pull. Tongue, gills, and all the intestines will come out through the belly slit. Sever them with a shallow cut around the ori-

# How to Clean a Fish

Make first cut with point of knife inside fish's mouth. Sever the narrow strip of gristle which joins the gills to the head.

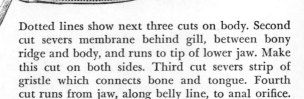

Dotted lines show next three cuts on body. Second cut severs membrane behind gill, between bony ridge and body, and runs to tip of lower jaw. Make this cut on both sides. Third cut severs strip of gristle which connects bone and tongue. Fourth cut runs from jaw, along belly line, to anal orifice.

Hook the finger through the bottom of the gill cut, around the tongue, and give a quick, sharp pull. Tongue, gills, and intestines will come out through belly slit. Clean blood from back vein by running thumb along backbone, then wash and wipe dry.

To help in making the belly cut the right depth, grind a wide V ⅛ to ¼ inch from tip of knife, sharpen with a hook hone.

# Cleaning a Fish from the Back

Insert knife tip just ahead of gill line until it hits bone (about ½ inch). Cut along both sides of the dorsal fin, as close to spines as possible.

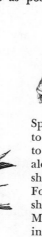

Spread cut with one hand to expose joinings of ribs to backbone. Cut the ribs along the backbone with a sharp knife if fish is small. For a large fish, use poultry shears or wire cutters. Make first three cuts shown in drawing on facing page, but don't make belly cut. Remove the gills from slit on back after cutting ribs.

Spread the fish, as shown, and remove the backbone and dorsal fin from the body. To do this, cut along each rib, grab the exposed rib tip with pliers, and twist it out.

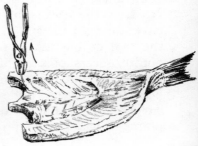

fice. Run your thumb along the backbone inside the cavity to remove the blood-filled back vein, and the fish is cleaned, ready to be washed and wiped dry. This method takes thirty seconds to one minute—a lot less time than it has taken you to read these directions. You might not clean your first fish in thirty seconds, but speed will come with a little practice.

There is only one point at which you might find it necessary to vary the procedure. On really big fish, the inner membrane along the backbone at the top of the cavity might be too tough to break with the pressure of a thumb. When cleaning big fish, make a slice the length of this membrane and use a narrow rubber spatula or a teaspoon to scrape the blood from along the backbone. This will be necessary only on fish of 10 pounds or more.

**Cleaning fish from the back.** When fish are to be smoked or plank-broiled, and especially when they are to be boned and stuffed, cleaning from the back is desirable. This is especially true when fish are to be plank-broiled or smoked; if cleaned from the belly they cannot be opened flat because of the thickness of back flesh and the presence of backbone and ribs. There is no quick, clean way to open a fish from the back, but the job is easier if you have the right tools: a very sharp knife, and in the case of big fish, a pair of kitchen shears, poultry shears, pointed tinsnips, or wire cutters.

Start by cutting along the backbone from head to tail, down to the bone; then spread the cut with your fingers until you can get the points of whatever snipping tool you are using around the first rib. Cut each rib close to the backbone, and with each cut the job grows easier. It will be messy, because no matter how careful you are, you'll cut into the blood-filled area at the top of the cavity. Mop the blood out and keep cutting.

When you have severed all the ribs, the cavity can be spread open. If the fish is to be planked, remove head, gills, and intestines at this point; they will come out easily through the wide-open back. The anal intestine is removed by cutting around the orifice to remove the vent and intestine as one unit. If you're stuffing the fish and want to leave the head intact, there's a bit more work involved, but you do have a better-looking dish to bring to the table. But the worst part of the job's already been done; the chances are that you punctured that blood-filled kidney area along the spine while you were cutting the ribs free. So just slice a little deeper, cut the membrane between kidney and intestinal cavity, and then turn the fish on its back to drain and wipe it clean, so you can see what you're doing.

Go in with the point of your knife at the top and back of the mouth and cut the strip of gristle, described earlier, that joins gills and teeth to the head. Make the back-of-the-gill cuts also described earlier, then pull out the gills from the back and cut the anal orifice out. After doing this, it's simple to remove the backbone and dorsal fin from the body. Cut along each rib, grab the exposed rib tip with pliers and twist it out. You may have to help this step with a touch of your knife point to avoid pulling too much flesh away with the rib. On fish like bass or trout, with a relatively simple bone structure, it's not a difficult job. On very bony fish such as shad or carp, it's a job to be avoided unless you've simply got to do it.

**Scale your fish** after they've been cleaned, not before. The job is much easier; after cleaning, for some reason, the scales seem to let go more readily. Scaling is necessary for almost all fish except trout, which have scales so small that they are virtually nonexistent. If you fish often and successfully, there are several devices that will make the scaling job easier. One is a rubber cylinder with hundreds of nubbins studding its surface; this chucks into an electric drill and takes the labor out of removing scales, once you've mastered the light touch its use requires. Another is a grooming-comb used by dog trainers, which is round, like a currycomb, but with much finer teeth. It, too, calls for a gentle touch.

Simplest of all scaling aids for any fish weighing over a couple of pounds, and if you're working where piped water is available, is a garden hose. Adjust the nozzle to a solid jet, hold the tip of the nozzle about three inches above the fish at a very sharp angle, almost horizontally, and apply the stream in even sweeps from tail to head. Do this with the fish laid out flat on your lawn and let the scales fly; they'll fall between the blades of grass and in time will dissolve and make excellent fertilizer. Change your working area after each fishing trip, and get rid of your spreader. Bury the intestines in your garden or flower beds, and they'll do

Rubber cylinder with studs on surface fits in drill chuck and speeds job of fish scaling.

Grooming-comb used by dog trainers makes a good scaler. It requires a light touch.

Fish over two pounds can be quickly scaled with the jet from a garden hose. Hold the tip of the nozzle three inches from the fish at a sharp angle. Apply stream in even sweeps from tail to head.

more for your plants than ten times their weight in chemical soil conditioners or fertilizers. But don't bury the fish heads—on page 33, you'll see why.

## Filleting

Fish that are to be filleted need not be cleaned or scaled, if you do the filleting soon after the fish is killed. To fillet, lay the fish on a solid surface, a wide cutting board, and cut just behind the gills at right angles to the body with a downward cut, until your knife touches the backbone. Hold the fish firmly by the head, turn the knife blade in the cut until it is parallel to the cutting surface and slide it with long, even sawing strokes along the backbone and ribs to the tail. Turn the fish over and repeat on the other side. Place the fillets on the cutting board, flesh side down, and slip the knife blade under the skin at the narrow end. When you've loosened an inch or so of skin, start rolling the skin into a cylinder, working toward the unskinned portion of the fillet. Cut in short, sawing strokes, rolling the skin back just ahead of the knife blade. The pressure of your left hand rolling the skin will hold the fillet firm while you're cutting skin from flesh.

There is only one secret to filleting a fish: your knife must be extremely sharp. Its blade should be no wider than ¾ inch. There are a number of good filleting knives on the market, but without prejudice to any manufacturer, choose a knife with a drop-forged, carbon-steel blade. Though stainless steels have been improved in recent years, knives of stainless steel

# How to Fillet a Fish

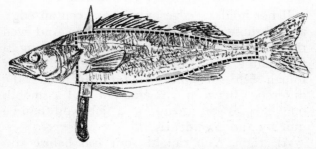

Lay fish on a cutting board and cut just behind the gills at right angles to the body, until knife touches backbone. Holding the fish firmly by the head, turn knife blade in the cut until it's parallel with board, and saw along backbone to the tail. (Dotted lines show both cuts.) Turn fish over and repeat.

Filleting cut shown in top view. By keeping the knife sliding along the backbone, and using a sawing cut, a fillet about the size shown by dotted lines will be removed.

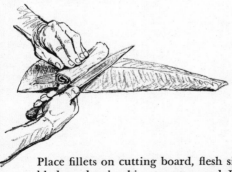

Place fillets on cutting board, flesh side down. Slip blade under the skin at narrow end. Loosen an inch or so of skin, then roll skin into a cylinder and with short, sawing strokes cut the skin from the flesh.

will not hold an edge or take as keen an edge, as will those with carbon-steel blades. And even the best blade should be whisked along a sharpening steel after about every third or fourth fish you fillet. Doing this makes the difference between a ragged cut and a smooth one, a job you dread or a job you handle quickly and confidently.

All right. You caught your fish before you opened the book, and now you've cleaned them. Let's go to the kitchen.

# 2

## UTENSILS AND INGREDIENTS

Although every ounce of flesh on the body of a fish is technically classified as muscle, there is no such thing as a tough fish. The only time you will ever sink your teeth into a tough piece of fish is when you bite into one that has not been properly cooked.

There is a basic difference between cooking fish and red meats, due to a basic difference in tissue. Red meats are made up of long strings of fiber gathered into bundles with tubes of connective tissue; under a microscope, a cross-section of red meat looks like strands of red spaghetti wrapped in a bundle with a piece of plastic. The flesh of fish is made up of short strands of fiber laid side by side in overlapping crescents; under a microscope it resembles a shingled roof.

This accounts for the difference in the approach you must use in cooking the two types. In red-meat cooking, you must expose the flesh to heat long enough to break down and tenderize both fibers and connective tissue. In fish cooking, you must expose the flesh to heat only long enough to coagulate the body liquids.

This does not mean that a fish can't be cooked in liquids other than those contained in its own body. Quite the contrary happens to be true. Fish poached in broth, water, wine, or any number of other liquids are not only delicious, but a welcome change from skillet-cooked or fried fish. So are fish baked whole,

19

with or without stuffing, and those prepared on the broiler or grill. There are many fine fish stews, soups and chowders. In cooking fish by any method, you can enhance its own flavor by the careful use of seasonings and by adding ingredients that will transfer a portion of their flavor to the fish.

But, by whatever method you cook, your basic objective remains the same. By the time a fish has been exposed to heat long enough to coagulate its juices, its flesh is completely cooked and at the peak of its flavor for eating. Any further application of heat does nothing but make the fish tough, dry, and stringy. This is true of all fish, regardless of its species. The old saying, "Let him stew in his own juice," is the best description of what fish cookery is all about.

## Utensils

Because of this basic objective, there are certain requirements for utensils used and processes followed in cooking fish. Let's face it; the worst enemy of good fish cooking is the thin, pressed-metal frying pan. If you feel that this statement casts unfair aspersions on your favorite cooking utensil, I'm sorry, but not apologetic. Skillets or frying pans of thin, pressed metal have two major flaws. The first is that they get too hot, regardless of the heat-source used, and the result is a fish with an undercooked center under a thin, overcooked outer layer and a charred skin. The second drawback of this type of pan is that it tends to develop hot spots, so that some parts of a fish are overcooked and other adjacent parts underdone. Fish are almost as sensitive as eggs to uneven heat distribution.

**Cast-iron skillets.** For sautéing—or frying, if you prefer to call it that—the best skillet is one of heavy cast iron, the kind grandma used. Second choice is the modernized version of grandma's standby; the skillet made of thin cast iron with a porcelain finish fused

Cast-iron skillet is best for sautéing fish.

to it. Either of these skillets will reward you with a better job of cooking, whether used over open coals, gas, or an electric element. If most of your cooking is done indoors, ceramic or glass utensils will prove almost as satisfactory as cast iron from the standpoint of providing a constant, controllable, low to medium temperature, and giving even heat distribution. The only drawback of glass and ceramic pans is that they are available only in small sizes.

**You can poach fish** in any utensil that is long enough to hold the whole fish. If water was the only liquid used for poaching, any roasting pan or Dutch oven or even a large, deep skillet would be satisfactory. However, all of these require a substantial quantity of liquid to cover the fish, and if the liquid happens to be wine or a special *court-bouillon*, this gets expensive.

Special fish poacher is designed to cook with a minimum of liquid.

There are special fish poachers designed to do this job with a minimum of liquid, and are more convenient to use than any of the alternate utensils already named. They are long, narrow, deep pans equipped with a perforated rack that has handles extending upward, by which the rack can be lifted out with the fish on it, intact.

In large cities, any housewares store can supply you with a fish poacher. If you live far from city shopping, you can order by mail from several sources. Bon Apetit, 113 South Nineteenth Street, Philadelphia, Pa. 19103, stocks poachers in three sizes, from 16 to 24 inches; the smallest size is $19.50. Alexander Sales, 26 South 6th Avenue, Mount Vernon, N. Y. 10551, lists a 14-inch and an 18-inch poacher; the small size is priced at $10.95. Colonial Garden, 270 West Merrick Road, Valley Stream, Long Island, N. Y. 11582, lists a 16-inch poacher at $19.95. If you feel like improvising, Maid Of Scandinavia, 3245 Raleigh Avenue, Minneapolis, Minn. 55416, has a narrow cake pan that can be used as a poacher; it is 17 inches long, its catalog number is 40010, and it is priced at $4.70. With this pan you must improvise your own rack or wrap your fish in cheesecloth to lift it out intact; a cover can be bent from heavy foil. A fish poacher, as you can see, is a rather specialized investment, and whether you equip yourself with one or use a pan already on your shelf is a matter between you and your budget.

**For baking fish,** any roasting pan does a good job. The essential requirements are a well-fitted cover and a rack that will fit into the pan and hold the fish about ½ inch to ¾ inch off its bottom. If you plan to do a lot of outdoor fish baking, over coals, your best bet is a Dutch oven. This means the genuine article, not the pans with plastic or wooden handles or glass tops accepted as Dutch ovens by the inexperienced and unwary. The Dutch oven you want for baking outdoors is cast iron throughout, handles and all, with a well-fitted dished metal top—a utensil that can be buried completely in the coals.

As for the sealed-tight earthenware utensils that are being widely publicized, they are excellent for everything except fish. Fish should never be cooked in a tightly-sealed container;

Dutch oven is best for baking fish outdoors over coals.

this includes both pressure cookers and tightly-crimped foil wrappings. Steam from a cooking fish must be allowed to escape, otherwise the flesh will reabsorb the steam's moisture and when cooked will be like canned salmon: soggy, soft, and tasteless.

These earthenware utensils bring to mind the legends about cooking fish encased in clay. This does work with the clays found in some localities, but clays differ widely. All mud is not clay, and unless you are an expert on soil composition or have an unlimited number of fish with which to experiment, wrap your fish in something else. The technique is quite simple, and although corn husks are most often used, other leaves such as lettuce are suitable. If fresh corn husks are to be the wrapping, use them just as shucked from the ear; encase your fish in a half-dozen layers and secure the wrapping with a spiral of thin wire. Bury them in the coals and leave them alone. Cooking time for an 8-inch fish will be 35 to 40 minutes; bigger fish take proportionately longer. If thin leaves, such as lettuce, are used, put a half-dozen layers around the fish and top this with eight or ten thicknesses of wet paper. The secret of cooking fish—or any other food—in coals is to use a porous wrapping that will allow steam to escape; otherwise, your food is not baked, but steamed.

**Grills.** If you are going to do a lot of grilling or broiling, the type of cooking generally and inaccurately called "barbecuing," a basket grill is one of the handiest accessories you can acquire. This type of grill is not a basket, but a pair of flat grids hinged together along one side, with a long handle on the other side, and a device to lock the two halves together. The fish is placed between the hinged sections, and the sections are closed and locked in place. The fish can then be turned simply by reversing the entire grill, without breaking its flesh. Basket grills, rectangular or in oval, fish-like shapes, can be found in most stores featuring outdoor cookware—or you can order them from

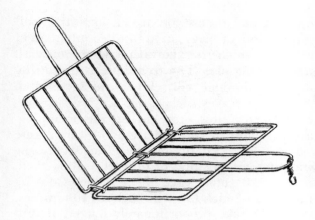

Basket grill for outdoor grilling and broiling.

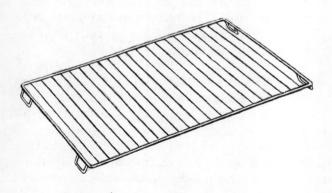

Oyster grill has closely spaced rods which support
fish and prevent it from breaking.

Electric *roti* cooks fish on both sides at once, reduces cooking time.

Spatula with offset blade is useful for cooking fish.

the sources given on page 23. Prices range from $5 to $9, depending on the size of the grill.

Another accessory useful in outdoor grilling and indoor broiling is what the hardware trade calls an "oyster grill." It is a grill with a small diameter and lightweight rods, closely spaced. Its chief virtue is that whole fish or fillets cooked on it hold their shape better and do not break as readily when being removed—as they do when cooked on a grill with thick, wide-spaced bars. Hardware and houseware stores and restaurant supply firms generally stock these grills. They are used by simply laying them on top of a regular grill.

Long a stand-by of European chefs is the *roti*, or vertical grill, a U-shaped device with mesh compartments on both sides to hold live coals. Food is placed in a basket grill, slipped in the center of the U, and cooked on both sides at once, which means much shorter cooking time. Recently, electric versions of the *roti* have come on the market; they use elements like those in a toaster, but much heavier. If you cannot locate one locally, the Country Kitchen, 270 West Merrick Road, Valley Stream, Long Island, N. Y. 11582, lists the grill at about $20.00, and Alexander Sales, 26 South 6th Avenue, Mount Vernon, N. Y. 10551, has a slightly different model at about $50.00.

**Tongs and a pair of spatulas** or turners are among the handiest accessories a fish cook can own. Tongs make it possible to turn small fish on the grill, in the skillet, or under the broiler, and to add or remove fish or pieces of fish in deep-fat frying. The ideal spatula for the fish chef is that called variously a "pastry cook's cake lifter" or a "fry cook's turner." It is an oversized pancake turner with an offset blade about 3 inches wide and 8 inches long. Use a pair to turn or lift big fish; slide the fish onto one, hold it firmly with the other, and the fish can be handled without danger of breaking or dropping. If local stores do not stock these, Maid Of Scandinavia, 3245 Raleigh Avenue, Minneapolis, Minn. 55416, lists a small model as #40738 in their catalog and a larger, heavy-duty model as #51373. The price of the small one is 49¢; the big one is $2.45. Remember, you will need a pair to do the job efficiently.

## Fats and Oils

For cooking purposes, all fish fall into one of two categories: lean and fat. Freshwater fish in the lean division are all pan fish and sunfish, black bass, muskellunge, pickerel, pike, catfish and whitefish; in this group, too, are the rough fish such as carp and suckers. Classified as fat are all the trout family, grayling, landlocked striped bass, and the anadromous fish: salmon, steelhead, shad and sturgeon. In simplest terms, the classification is based on the quantity of oil contained in the tissues—and this is important to the cook.

In some species, such as trout, this oil is very delicate and has little or no effect on the taste of the cooked fish. However, in such big fish as anadromous species and the landlocked striper, the oil is strong and plentiful. When these fish are cooked by a method that allows oil to be retained or reabsorbed by the flesh, the flavor may be altered in a very unfortunate way.

Generally speaking, fat fish are best when broiled, grilled, baked, or poached. Pan-cooking allows the oil to be reabsorbed, since the fish is bathed in it while in the pan; and when modified by heat, the oil becomes quite unsavory. When the fish is cooked on a grill or broiler rack, or baked on a rack in a roasting pan, the oil drains away. In poaching, the liquid in which the fish is cooked will counteract the taste of the oil, diluting its effect so that it is not objectionable.

If you doubt that this makes a difference, test it out. Pan-fry a steak or fillet from a large fat fish and broil or grill an identical cut from the same fish, seasoning both portions identically. Taste and compare, and you will quickly be convinced. Don't dismiss this as a mere trifle. Perhaps it is, but such trifles are what make the difference between excellent and mediocre cooking.

So far, we've devoted a lot of attention to trifles, but it hasn't been attention wasted. I have a theory about cooking from recipes. Simply writing down a series of ingredients and instructions doesn't necessarily convince the cook of the need to follow directions. It's like saying, "Do this because I tell you to." Any cook worth his (or her) salt and spices wants to know why those directions are given, and when provided with a sensible reason for them, follows the recipe.

We're finally ready to start cooking. First, let's consider the medium in which your fish will be cooked. It may be none at all, as in the case of baked fish. Or, it may be an oil or fat, a broth or stock, plain water, or the mixture of water, wine and seasonings that is called *court-bouillon*. Especially in fish cookery, the cooking medium becomes an integral part of the seasoning—an important aid in arriving at the desired flavor.

Quite a number of angler-chefs associate fish with the flavor of bacon, since bacon dripping is the fat most commonly used in camp cooking. Its use gives fish a very pronounced flavor, which is not always desirable if the fish is to be served with a sauce. Relatively few sauces benefit by the introduction of bacon flavor, and the use of a neutral cooking fat is recommended when sautéed fish are to be sauced. However, if you are one of those who feels disadvantaged if your pan-cooked fish lacks that bacon taste, by all means use bacon dripping and nothing more than salt and pepper for seasoning. But, if you seek variety of taste, switch to other oils or fats.

Inevitably, the search for neutral cooking fats leads to the oils. Most vegetable oils come from corn, which yields an unsaturated fat. But most corn oils now contain a foam retardant made from silicone, and many people frown upon the idea of cooking in a fat that contains the basic ingredient of synthetic rubber, hydraulic fluid and varnish. This leaves us with the pure, unadulterated oils: olive, peanut, and safflower.

For many years I have used a light olive oil in dishes where its flavor enhances the final result, and a pure peanut oil where I want a neutral fat with no flavor of its own. For top-of-stove cooking, especially for sautéing fish, my first choice is peanut oil. This oil does not break down at high temperatures, it does not absorb the flavors of foods cooked in it and re-transmit them to other foods, and it does not turn rancid even when kept unrefrigerated for long periods. For deep-fat frying, with its higher temperatures, I find that a mixture of ⅓ solid fat and ⅔ peanut oil gives very satisfactory results.

Butter remains first choice when cooking fish that are to be sauced; there is no sauce with which butter is not compatible. To avoid smoking, sputtering and excessive browning of foods, sauté with drawn butter. Its preparation is simple: heat butter in a small saucepan at a very low temperature until its oils and solids separate; then, remove the pan from heat and let it stand until the white solids settle to the bottom. Carefully pour off the liquid fat, and you have drawn butter—also called clarified butter.

Margarines are commonly substituted for butter by those seeking to avoid animal fats, and this is fine if you choose a margarine free from coconut oil. The "soft" margarines should be avoided in cooking; they contain chemicals which prevent them from blending properly with the acid liquids such as lemon juice, vinegar and wine, which are called for in many recipes and in most sauces. Even some of the solid margarines now contain softening chemicals to make them easier to spread when cold, but which effectively prevent them from blending with acids. In recipes where substitutes can be made, it will be noted.

The type of liquid to be used when poaching fish will also be specified, and any alternates that can be used without altering the flavor of the finished dish will be given. Liquids used in poaching are plain water, water modified with herbs or seasonings, or the traditional fish stock or *court-bouillon*. Fish stock uses the heads, bones and scraps of flesh left after trimming; this is why you were warned not to use fish heads for fertilizer a few pages back. The preparation of stock and *court-bouillon* is very simple, and these liquids should be used in poaching wherever indicated in recipes. And in Chapter 12 you will find a few suggestions on wines used in cooking and serving fish dishes.

## Seasoning

If you enjoy eating fish—and some fishermen don't, because they mistreat their catch either in pre-cooking care or in the cooking itself—then you like the flavor of a well-turned trout, bass or catfish or whatever has taken your hook. The next assumption we'll make is that since you do enjoy the flavor of fish, you don't want that flavor smothered by overly-heavy seasonings or sauces. Good. We're talking the same language. Using fish as the base of a heavily-spiced dish such as chili would be about as sensible as using cornflakes. Come to think of it, a highly-seasoned dish like chili would taste about the same if fish or cornflakes were used in it instead of red meat.

There are several herbs and spices traditionally associated with fish. The major herbs are dill, fennel, thyme, marjoram, sorrel and tarragon; the minor ones are rosemary, basil and oregano. The root herbs chiefly used are onions, shallots, and garlic—and don't frown at the onion being classed as a root herb. Purists may not give them herb status, but if we classify according to use, the onion deserves to be considered with the herbs. The principal spice you will use is pepper, with paprika following.

When you buy herbs and spices for cooking, do yourself a favor and get fresh herbs and whole spices. Use the pre-ground packaged kind as a last resort; even in sealed containers, ready-ground herbs and spices deteriorate quickly and you have no way of knowing how long they've been on the grocer's shelf. Anderson Farm, Tinicum, Pipersville, Pa. 18947, can supply most herbs in fresh form and dried whole herbs with full potency.

Almost all herbs and spices get their characteristic flavors from extremely volatile oils, and grinding or crushing liberates them. The difference in flavor between freshly-ground or crushed seasonings and those that have been standing for a long time in prepared form is tremendous. Pepper is perhaps the most notable example. For appearance as well as flavor, I prefer to use white pepper and grind it as needed. You will probably tire of seeing the phrase "freshly-ground white pepper" in the recipes that follow, but don't knock it until you've tried it. Invest a couple of dollars in a peppermill and a supply of fresh white peppercorns and test the difference yourself.

In most fish recipes, the theory that "if a little bit is good, a lot is better" can't be applied. It's the cooking equivalent of casting for trout in a small mountain stream with flies tied on shark hooks. Admittedly, a number of the roughfish require substantial seasoning to make them really tasty, but in most dishes the fish itself should provide the flavor and not just serve as a vehicle for the seasonings cooked with it. Keeping in mind what your own taste dictates in seasoning, use a light hand and let the flavor of the fish make the dish.

It was, if memory serves correctly, the Greek historian Herodotus who first put into writing the aphorism, "Food should taste like what it really is." This is as true today as when it was first written, in about 450 B. C., and it would be well to keep the phrase in mind when you get out the pots and heat up the stove.

# 3

## BASIC FISH COOKERY

Since the journey of a thousand miles begins with a single step, that first step is pretty important. Here, the first step is to become acquainted with the six basic ways in which fish are cooked, and the variations in those six ways. It's possible that you know all six methods by heart, and what this chapter contains might be merely a repetition of something with which you're thoroughly familiar, but please don't skip it. There just may be something in it that will be new to you. After all, there's not any way to avoid taking that first step. In spite of all our technological advances, we've got to walk to the car or the plane, and even to the rocket that lifts us off to the moon.

By whatever method you cook your fish, keep in mind the objective of all fish cookery: to cook only long enough to coagulate the juices. If a fish was shaped like a slab, this wouldn't be difficult. However, since fish taper from thick to thin, we must seek a happy medium. Take your fish off the fire while the thickest part is still quite moist. Cooking will continue by retained heat for several moments after you transfer the fish from the pan to a warmed plate or platter. In actual practice, cooking should be completed during the time required to take the fish out of the pan, put it on a plate, and carry it to the table—usually, a matter of 3 or 4 minutes. If you err in timing, it is better to undercook than to overcook.

Your clues to the point at which a fish is done are the condition of its skin and the amount of moisture at its dorsal fin. When cooking is completed, the skin will slip easily from the flesh. Usually, the side that is up will show a few large air bubbles between skin and flesh. The slipping quality of the skin can be tested at the slit cut for cleaning, or where the dorsal fin has been trimmed along the back. Test with a knife tip or the tines of a fork, and if the skin lifts readily, the fish is done.

Use a knife or fork to make the dorsal fin test, too. Slip the utensil into the skinless line left where the fin was cut off. Twist the blade or tines gently to separate the flesh; if no liquid flows, but the flesh has a moist appearance, cooking is complete. By the time you've taken the fish off the broiler rack or grill, or out of the skillet, and laid it on a hot plate, it should be possible to tweak out the dorsal spines. Usually you can do this with your fingers, pinching the spines through a folded cloth to protect your fingers and give you a better grip. Stubbornly-rooted spines, especially in big fish, may have to be pulled out with pliers.

Few fish are skinned before cooking. The chief exceptions are catfish and fillets taken from big fish. When small fish are served, either pan-fried or in a mixed dish such as a stew, it's usually up to the person eating them to remove skin and bones from his own portion. Often, though, the cook will want to remove the skin from a large baked or poached fish that's going to be served whole, and sometimes it's desirable to remove the backbone and ribs as well.

The easy way to do this is to slip the skin off the side that's uppermost while the fish is still on the rack or in the pan in which it was cooked. Then, invert the platter and lay it on the fish; hold rack, fish and platter firmly and turn the whole thing over; lift off the rack, and slip off the skin from the unskinned side, which is now uppermost.

To divide the flesh of a large cooked fish into halves, like big fillets, the skin should be removed first. Then, insert a dull knife at the thickest part of the body, behind the head, and cut along the dorsal line, with the tip of the knife touching the backbone. Work the edge of a turner or metal spatula into the cut and push and lift very gently, keeping the edge of the tool against the ribs and inching along the backbone from head to tail with the spatula while pushing the slab of flesh toward the belly. By working slowly and carefully, you can remove the slab of flesh in one piece, after which it is a simple matter to lift out the exposed backbone with the ribs attached. A few ribs may stick in the bottom half, but they can be loosened with a nick of the knife; if they break, they can be tweaked out.

Your success in doing this depends to a large extent on the fish having been cooked properly; if it is overdone and dry, even a light touch will cause the flesh to separate and break. And don't try this method of separation with exceedingly bony fish such as carp, shad and pike. It's far better to serve them whole or in sections cut at right angles to the body, and let each diner remove the bones from his own portion.

One more generality. As different as the families of fish are, they have more similarities than differences. As a result, they are largely interchangeable in pan or pot. Although the bulk of this book is divided into chapters dealing with the principal families of fish, different species can be quite freely interchanged. There are only a few recipes in which substitution of one kind of fish for another is either impossible or ill-advised, and when this is the case, a word of caution will be given.

Now, cook and enjoy. If Allah does not deduct from man's alloted life span the time he spends at fishing, the moments devoted to cooking the fish should be equally exempt.

## Pan-Frying or Sautéing

This is the only method of cooking fish that many people know of or use. The name "pan-frying" is given to this style of cooking to distinguish it from true frying, which is done in a deep pot with the food totally immersed in hot fat. Technically, we are talking in this section about sautéing, which does not mean plopping a fish into a pan half-filled with fat and browning the outside in the shortest possible time over the highest possible heat. Do that and your fish will have a tooth-shattering crust surrounding a half-raw interior. Use moderate heat, and coat the fish with an ingredient or combination of ingredients that hold it off the bottom of the pan so the fat can get underneath it. Cook it long enough to allow the heat to penetrate even the thickest part and you'll serve up an evenly-cooked morsel.

## Camp Style Sautéing

**Whole fish no thicker than 2 to 2½ inches at the thickest part, or fillets**

**Cooking fat: oil, bacon, dripping, butter, solid margarine, lard, as you prefer**

**Breading ingredients: cornmeal, fine dry breadcrumbs, or fine unsalted cracker crumbs in quantity depending on the number of fish to be cooked**

Have enough fat to cover the bottom of the skillet to a depth of ¼ inch to ½ inch for whole fish, and to a depth of no more than $\frac{1}{16}$ inch to ⅛ inch for fillets. The fat should be well below the smoking point, the heat moderate. Roll the fish in the breading ingredient, covering its outside surfaces thoroughly. Cook whole fish 2 to 4 minutes per side, depending upon thickness; reduce heat and extend cooking time for thick-bodied fish. Test for doneness by methods given on page 37. Drain the fish for a moment on cloth or paper towels before serving, and do not salt until cooking is completed.

## American Style Sautéing

**Whole fish no thicker than 2 to 2½ inches at the thickest part, or fillets**

**Cooking fat: oil, bacon dripping, butter, solid margarine, lard, as you prefer**

**Milk or evaporated milk diluted with equal parts water; the quantity will depend on the number of fish being cooked**

**Flour; the quantity will depend on the number of fish being cooked**

Have enough fat to cover the bottom of the skillet to a depth of ¼ inch to ½ inch for whole fish, and to a depth of no more than ¹⁄₁₆ inch to ⅛ inch for fillets. The fat should be well below the smoking point, the heat moderate. Dip the fish in milk, drain for a moment, then roll in flour. Shake off any excess flour, but be sure all outside surfaces of the fish are covered. Cook whole fish 2 to 4 minutes per side, depending upon thickness; fillets, 2 minutes per side. Use lower heat and extend cooking time for thick-bodied fish. Test for doneness by methods given on page 37. Drain the fish on cloth or paper towels before serving. Do not season until after cooking.

## English Style Sautéing

Whole fish no thicker than 2 to 2½ inches at the thickest part, or fillets

Cooking fat: oil, bacon dripping, butter, solid margarine, lard, as you prefer

Flour; the quantity will depend on the number of fish being cooked

Coating: 1 egg, 1 tablespoon milk, 1 tablespoon cooking oil, ½ teaspoon salt; this will handle a half-dozen panfish, four fillets, or two 8-inch whole fish. Mix any quantity needed, using the ratio given above

Fine dry breadcrumbs; the quantity will depend on the number of fish being cooked

Have enough fat to cover the bottom of the skillet to a depth of ¼ inch to ½ inch for whole fish, and to a depth of no more than ¹⁄₁₆ inch to ⅛ inch for fillets. The fat should be well below the smoking point, the heat moderate to low. Whole fish cooked this style are often "crimped," that is, slashed across the body on each side with three or four deep cuts; this is supposed to keep the fish from curling in the pan while cooking, but whether you follow the custom or not is up to you. Wipe the fish with a damp cloth and roll in flour, rubbing it in well. Dip the fish in the coating liquid and let it drain for a moment; then roll in bread-crumbs, covering the outside surfaces thoroughly. Cook whole fish 4 to 7 minutes per side, depending upon thickness; cook fillets about 4 minutes per side. Use lower heat and extend cooking time for large fish. Determine when cooking is completed by methods given on page 37. Drain on cloth or paper towels for a moment before serving.

## Deep-Fat Frying

We turn now to true frying, which is done in a deep pan with the fish completely immersed in hot fat. The process is best suited to small fish cooked whole, or to large fish that have been cut into pieces of approximately equal size. The pieces or the small whole fish should not be seasoned before being cooked unless the seasoning is included in a breading or coating. The coating may be any of those given in the preceding recipes for sautéing, although you will find the plain coating of cornmeal or fine dried breadcrumbs to be the most satisfactory.

There are three keys to success in this style of cooking. The first is the composition of the fat used; ⅓ solid shortening to ⅔ cooking oil is the preferred ratio. The second is the temperature of the cooking fat; if you have a cooking thermometer, 370 to 380 degrees is the ideal. At this temperature the inside of small whole fish or pieces about 1 inch to 1¼ inch large will be completely cooked and the outside crisply browned in 5 minutes. The third secret is to add the fish or pieces a few at a time to keep the temperature of the cooking fat constant.

Use a large pan and do not overcrowd it. Bring the fat to smoking temperature, if you have no cooking thermometer, then reduce heat until the smoking stops. Put in and remove the fish or pieces with tongs. Drain the cooked fish on cloth or paper towels for a moment before serving.

## Broiling and Grilling

To be technical for a moment, broiling is done with the fish or fillets on a rack placed in a shallow pan with the heat source above the fish; heat reflected from the bottom of the broiling pan will generally cook the bottom side so that the fish need not be turned. Grilling is done with the fish on a rack or grill with the heat source beneath it; the heat is usually from live coals, and the fish must be turned at half the cooking time. Another type of broiling is that done in a *roti,* or vertical grill, described on page 28.

When broiling, the broiler as well as the rack and pan should be preheated for at least 5 minutes. Each broiler is unique. Even kitchen ranges manufactured on a production line, using identical components, will vary slightly. Thermostatic devices designed to maintain heat at a uniform level will show similar variation. This is as true of gas broilers as it is of electric broilers. A good rule of thumb is to use three-quarters heat with gas, full heat with electricity. Cook the fish with its top surface 6 to 7 inches from the heat source; the approximate cooking time for a fish 1½ to 2 inches thick at the thickest part will be about 10 minutes. Use the tests on page 37 to determine when cooking is completed.

There are even more variables in grilling. Air currents, depth of the coals, distance of the grill rack from them, all play a part in altering your timing. In this style of cooking, about the only advice I can offer is to have a deep bed of coals, dark red rather than yellow-hot, and use the tests on page 37 to judge cooking time.

Fish broiled or grilled should be basted. Individual recipes will give specific basting mixtures, but a good all-purpose basting liquid can be made by mixing 2 parts oil or drawn butter with 1 part lemon or lime juice.

When cooking pieces of fish on a skewer, what is commonly called kabobing or shishkabobing, or cooking *en brochette,* marinate the pieces in lemon or lime juice for 45 minutes to 1 hour before cooking. This firms the flesh and makes it less likely to flake into pieces and fall off the skewers as cooking progresses. Fish of any kind, because of the layerlike formation of its flesh, is a poor candidate at best for this kind of cooking. Skewer-cook fish only when you are forced to do so; there are too many other kinds of meats better suited to this style of preparation.

## Baking

For baking whole, choose fish ranging in size from 4 or 5 pounds on up to about 10 or 12 pounds. These are really too small to yield steaks and too big to pan-fry; they should be baked, either stuffed or plain, or poached. Also good for baking are center cuts from fish ranging between 12 and 30 pounds, and roasts cut from giants such as the sturgeon.

Individual recipes for baking fish will give you the specific cooking time, since there will be a variation depending on the type of stuffing or dressing used. For plain, unadorned baked fish, cooked in a pre-heated 350-degree oven in an open pan, the rule of thumb is 7 minutes per inch of thickness at the thickest part; in a closed pan, 10 minutes per inch. This will be accurate within a minute either way, if your oven's thermostat is accurate, but use the tests on page 37 to be sure.

In open-pan baking, fish are generally basted, using the liquid given with individual recipes or the general-purpose basting liquid on page 44. Fat fish should always be cooked on a rack that will hold them ½ inch to ¾ inch from the bottom of the baking pan. Juices from the pan should not be used for basting: see page 30 if you've forgotten why.

# Poaching

This is what some call "boiling." Except for the traditional outdoor fish boils indigenous to the upper Midwest, fish should never really be boiled. They should be poached in a fish stock or in a *court-bouillon;* the recipes for both of these follow.

## Fish Stock

2 pounds fish trimmings: heads, bones with bits of flesh
2 medium-sized sweet onions sliced thin
5 or 6 large sprigs parsley
4 to 6 peppercorns, nicked or cracked
1½ pints cold water
1½ pints dry white wine (see page 178)
1 teaspoon salt

Rub a deep saucepan very lightly with cooking oil. Put in all the solid ingredients, cover the pan tightly, and cook 15 to 20 minutes over very low heat. Add liquids and salt, bring to a boil, reduce to a simmer, and cook 45 minutes with the pan uncovered. Strain or clarify (page 47) before putting into container with a well-fitting top for storage in refrigerator; the stock will keep for about 8 weeks. Makes 2 quarts.

## Court-Bouillon

1 quart dry white wine (see page 178)
2 quarts cold water
1½ cups minced sweet onion
1 cup peeled minced carrots

*Bouquet garni* composed of:
  4 pieces celery tops with leaves left on
  6 sprigs parsley
  1 bay leaf
  1 sprig fresh thyme or 2 sprigs dried thyme
  8 peppercorns, cracked or nicked with a knife blade

Put all ingredients except the peppercorns into a deep saucepan and bring to a brisk rolling boil. Reduce heat until the liquid simmers and cook 40 minutes, adding the peppercorns during the last 10 minutes. (If cooked too long in a thin liquid, peppercorns make it bitter.) Strain or clarify (page 47) before putting into a container with a well-fitting top for storage in refrigerator; the liquid will keep for about 8 weeks. Makes 2½ quarts.

### To Clarify Stock or Court-Bouillon

For each quart of liquid, beat one egg white until stiff and break one clean eggshell into large pieces. Heat the liquid, stir in the egg whites and shell, bring to a boil, remove from heat, and let stand 10 minutes. Strain into a clean container through a dampened, closely-woven cloth; flannel is best.

When poaching fish, it is usually desirable to start the cooking in a cool or lukewarm liquid, although there will be some variation in individual recipes. If you are using a poaching pan, simply put the fish on the rack and lower it into the liquid, which should cover it completely. If you do not own a special pan for poaching, use any container of suitable size, and wrap the fish loosely in three or four layers of cheese-cloth, leaving the ends long enough to use in lifting the fish from the pan when done.

After putting in the fish, bring the liquid to a boil. Then reduce heat until it barely simmers on the surface, the slowest simmering heat of which your stove is capable. Length of poaching time will vary with the size of the fish; a 4-pounder will require about 25 minutes from the time boiling stops. As a rule of thumb, cook 3 to 4 minutes for each pound over 4 pounds.

One more word about the liquids used in poaching. There is no substitute for *court-bouillon,* but you can use canned clam juice diluted with water as a substitute for fish stock. Keep in mind that there are two liquids canned from clams: juice and broth. The juice can be diluted with 3 parts water, the broth with 1½ to 2 parts water.

## Stews, Chowders, Soups

Each recipe for cooking fish in these styles will have a slightly different approach; it is only the style that is basic. All that can be done here is to encourage you to try some of the recipes.

So much for the basics, the reference points which apply to all methods of cooking fish. We're now ready to move to the recipes that transform fish, by combining them with sauces and other ingredients, into dishes even more delicious than they are when cooked in plain-Jane styles.

# 4

## PANFISH

There are, icthyologists tell us, between 35 and 40 different kinds of panfish distributed across the North American continent. Many of them are known by as many as three or four regional names, so that telling who the players are in the panfish game is a pretty tough job, even with a scorecard. Best known of the panfish are: perch, which have a half-dozen names in as many different areas; crappie, also known as croppie and chinquapins and striped sand-bass; bream, often called brim and sometimes warmouth; bluegill, which are also tagged with the names of dollardee, coppernose, chainside, blue perch and gold perch; punkinseed; redear; and so on down a long list. And all panfish answer to the name of sunfish as well.

Most panfish weigh a pound or less, but they are for the most part easily caught in quantities large enough to allow them to be served in adequate numbers. None of the panfish have any peculiarities that require special attention in cleaning, but one of their family characteristics is a light, delicate flavor that goes fast unless they are cleaned quickly after being taken from the water.

All panfish can be interchanged or mixed in any of the recipes in this chapter. You will, of course, let the average size of the fish determine the number you offer as an individual serving, but to be safe count on at least three or four fish per person. All panfish can be cooked by any of the basic recipes given in Chapter 3.

When pan-frying them or when frying them in deep fat, bury the fish in a big tub of cracked ice for 30 minutes before cooking and you will find their flavor greatly improved. When you poach them, be careful to avoid overcooking. Once the poaching liquid has boiled, remove the pan from heat and let it sit 5 minutes before taking out the fish and you will find them cooked to perfection.

### Crisped Panfish

**12 to 16 cleaned panfish**
**Large bowl or bucket of fine cracked ice**
**2 eggs, lightly beaten**
**¾ cup cornmeal**
**¾ cup flour**
**1½ teaspoons salt**
**Large dash pepper**
**½ to ¾ cup cooking fat or oil**

Bury the cleaned fish in ice for 30 minutes before cooking. Beat the eggs in a shallow bowl. Combine the cornmeal, flour and seasonings in a small plastic bag. Put enough cooking fat into a heavy skillet to cover the bottom to a depth of ¼ inch to ½ inch and bring it to medium-high heat. Take the fish from the ice a few at a time and wipe them dry. Dip them in the beaten egg, then roll them in the corn-meal-flour mixture until they are thoroughly coated. Drop them in the pan a few at a time; do not overcrowd the pan. Cook 2 minutes on each side. Drain well on cloth or paper towels. Keep the level of fat in the pan constant and its temperature even. Use one of the Quick Sauces given in Chapter 12. Serves 4.

## Panfish with Zucchini

10 to 12 panfish, pan-fried according to any
of the recipes given beginning on page 50
3 or 4 zucchini (green Italian squash) no
larger than 1-inch in diameter and 4 to 6
inches long
1 canned pimiento, drained, wiped dry, cut
in 1-inch strips
1 tablespoon cider vinegar

After cooking the fish, put them in a warmed,
covered bowl. Drain all but a light film of oil
from the skillet. Wash the zucchini, trim off the
ends, and slice at a very sharp angle, almost
lengthwise, into slices ¼ inch to ½ inch thick.
Sauté the zucchini in the oil remaining in the
skillet, cooking about 1 minute per side over
medium-high heat. Add the pimiento strips and
the fish, stir, cover the pan and leave it on the
heat just long enough to warm the fish. Remove
to a heated platter and sprinkle with the vinegar just before serving. (Lemon juice can be
used in place of vinegar if you prefer.) Serves 4.

## Panfish in Cider

12 to 16 cleaned panfish
1 large sweet onion, peeled and sliced very
thin
3 carrots, peeled or scraped, sliced lengthwise
into very thin strips
1 stalk celery cut into thin crosswise slices
2 quarts sweet cider
1 teaspoon salt
2 tablespoons butter or margarine
2 tablespoons flour

Put the vegetables into a deep cooking pot, lay the fish on top, and pour the cider over them. Add the salt. Bring to a boil and when boiling begins reduce to a simmer and cook for 5 minutes. At this point the fish should be removed with tongs or a slotted spoon and placed in a heated bowl. Let the vegetables continue simmering until the carrots are tender; this will be about 5 minutes. Remove the carrots, onions and celery, strain the cider, and return 1 quart to the pan. Boil briskly until it is reduced in volume by one-third, and reduce to a simmer. Blend butter and flour into a smooth paste and flake it in small bits into the cider, stirring until it dissolves. Return fish and vegetables to the pot long enough to reheat, about 2 minutes. Serve in a bowl or individual soup bowls with boiled potatoes or rice as a side dish. Serves 4 to 6.

## Panfish Portuguese Style

12 to 16 cleaned panfish
1½ cups fish stock (page 46)
1 cup canned tomato sauce
1 cup grated sweet onion
1 clove garlic, crushed or minced very fine
1 sweet red pepper, cleaned and diced fine
2 tablespoons chopped fresh parsley
1 teaspoon salt
1 cup dry red wine (a California Zinfandel is the nearest equivalent to the wine that would be used in Portugal)
1 tablespoon butter or margarine

Butter a large ovenproof dish quite generously and lay the fish in it loosely. Combine
the stock, tomato sauce, onion, garlic, pepper,
parsley and salt; pour this over the fish. Cook
uncovered in a preheated 320-degree oven for
10 minutes. Pour in the wine, flake the butter
over the top, and cook 10 minutes longer. Stir
before serving. Serves 4 to 6.

## Panfish with Vegetables

**12 to 16 cleaned panfish**
**Salt**
**Freshly-ground white pepper**
**3 tablespoons butter or margarine**
**2 large boiled potatoes, peeled, cut in juli-
enne strips**
**2 medium-sized sweet onions, peeled, sliced
½-inch thick with the slices separated into
rings**
**2 cups green peas, fresh, frozen, or canned**
**½ cup dry white wine**
**½ cup light cream, or evaporated milk di-
luted ⅔ milk, ⅓ water**

Dust the cavities of the fish generously with
salt and pepper and set them aside to rest for
10 to 15 minutes before putting into the pot.
If fresh green peas are used, they should be
parboiled 5 minutes in lightly-salted water.
Frozen peas should be dropped in boiling water
and left for 3 minutes after they thaw. Canned
peas need only be drained.

Melt 2 tablespoons of the butter in a large,
deep skillet having a tight-fitting cover. Over
medium-high heat, stir and toss the vegetables

in the butter until the onions begin to turn a light tan. Spread the vegetables into a layer on the bottom of the pan, lay the fish on them and put a small dot of butter on each. Pour in the wine, cover the pan, reduce heat to its lowest range and cook 15 minutes. Open the pan, pour in the cream, stir well. Close the pan for 5 more minutes of cooking and serve. Serves 4 to 6.

## Panfish with Shallots

    12 to 16 cleaned panfish
    6 cups *court-bouillon* (page 47); no substitutes)
    ¼ cup cider vinegar
    4 shallots, peeled and chopped coarsely (no substitutes)
    ¼ pound butter (no substitutes)
    2 tablespoons chopped fresh parsely

Have the cold *court-bouillon* in a deep pot, put the fish in and bring to a gentle boil. When boiling begins, reduce at once to a simmer and cook 5 minutes. When simmering begins, take ½ cup of the *court-bouillon* from the pot and put it in a small saucepan, add vinegar and shallots, bring quickly to a brisk boil and cook until the liquid is reduced to half its volume; stir occasionally to avoid scorching the shallots. When the liquid is reduced, lower heat to simmer and begin adding the butter by tablespoonsful, beating with a wire whisk or an old-style hand eggbeater between each addition to produce a frothy, creamy sauce. Then put the fish on a hot platter and pour the sauce over them; sprinkle with parsley. Serves 4.

## Panfish Bordeaux Style

2 tablespoons butter (no substitutes)
3 medium-sized sweet onions, peeled and sliced thin
¾ cup broken or coarsely-chopped walnut meats
1½ cups mushrooms, fresh or canned; if canned mushrooms are used, drain well
12 to 16 cleaned panfish
1½ teaspoons salt
Large dash freshly-ground white pepper
2 cups claret (see page 178)
1 cup fish stock (page 46)
¾ to 1 cup coarse fresh breadcrumbs
1 tablespoon grated Parmesan cheese
1½ to 2 tablespoons melted butter (no substitutes)

On top of the stove, sauté the onions in 2 tablespoons butter, using an ovenproof dish that can go to the table later. When the onions begin to turn golden, add the walnuts and mushrooms and stir well. Put the fish on top of the ingredients in the pan, sprinkle with the salt and pepper, combine the wine and fish stock and pour over them. Close the pan and transfer it to a preheated 300-degree oven. Cook for 20 minutes. Mix breadcrumbs, cheese and melted butter, open the dish and spread the breadcrumb mixture over the top. Put under the broiler one or two minutes, just long enough to brown the topping to a tasty golden tan. Serves 4 to 6.

## Panfish Fricassee

2 tablespoons butter or margarine
2 tablespoons flour
1½ cups fish stock (page 46)
1 cup dry white wine
¼ cup dry vermouth
1 anchovy fillet, drained and pulped (do not
    substitute anchovy paste; it is too coarse
    and too salty)
½ teaspoon salt
Moderate dash freshly-ground white pepper
3 carrots, peeled or scraped, sliced in paper-
    thin rounds
12 to 16 cleaned panfish

Melt the butter in a deep, heavy skillet. Add
the flour by sprinkling it over the butter evenly,
then stirring immediately and briskly to form
a smooth white paste, or *roux*. Cook over medium heat 3 or 4 minutes, but do let the *roux*
brown. Combine the fish stock, wine and vermouth and pour into the pan slowly and evenly
while stirring to form a smooth sauce. Stir in
the pulped anchovy and seasonings; add the
carrot and fish. Close the pan and simmer 10
to 12 minutes. If the sauce thickens too much,
stir in a little more stock; you want a sauce
just thicker than rich cream. Serves 4 to 6.

## Creamy Panfish Chowder

12 to 16 cleaned panfish
1 heart of celery with root stub and leaves,
    minced
2 small onions, peeled and chopped fine

1 bay leaf

2 teaspoons salt

3 or 4 peppercorns, cracked or nicked with a knife

3 large potatoes, peeled and sliced ½-inch thick

2 thick slices salt pork or fat bacon

1 cup heavy cream or undiluted evaporated milk

2½ cups milk or evaporated milk diluted with equal parts water

Oyster crackers

Put the fish in a deep pot and pour in 1½ quarts cold water, more if needed to cover them completely. Add the celery, onions, bayleaf, salt, and peppercorns. Bring to a boil, reduce to a simmer, and cook 5 minutes from the time simmering begins. Strain the broth into a saucepan, put in the potatoes, and bring to a bubbling boil. While the potatoes cook, remove the fish, skin them and flake the flesh from their bones, and put the flesh in a warmed bowl. Prepare the salt pork; its rinds should be trimmed off and the pork blanched by plunging it into boiling water for 3 minutes. (Bacon, if used in place of salt pork, need not be blanched.) Dice the salt pork and sauté until crisply browned. As soon as the potatoes become tender, add the pork, fish, milk, and cream to the pot; include the fat from the skillet in which the pork cooked. When the pot is simmering again, remove from heat and serve in soup bowls with crushed oyster crackers sprinkled on top. Serves 6 to 8.

## Panfish Burgundy Style

4 tablespoons butter or margarine
2 medium-sized sweet onions, peeled and
    sliced thin
12 to 16 cleaned panfish
½ teaspoon salt
Dash of freshly-ground white pepper
1½ cups Burgundy-type wine (see page 178)
1 tablespoon butter or margarine
1 tablespoon flour
1 tablespoon meat extract: Bovril, B. V., etc.

Sauté the onions in 4 tablespoons butter, using a pan that can be put into the oven. Cook until the onions become transparent, then lay the fish on the onions, dust with salt and pepper, and pour in the wine. Cover the pan and cook in a preheated 350-degree oven for 15 to 20 minutes. Remove the fish to heated serving plates or a platter. Strain the pan liquid into a saucepan. Combine 1 tablespoon butter and 1 tablespoon flour into a smooth paste and flake this into the simmering pan liquid over low heat, stirring each addition until it dissolves. Simmer 3 minutes after adding the last of the butter-flour paste, stir in the meat extract, and divide the sauce over the fish. Serves 4.

## Hot Panfish Salad

10 to 12 cleaned panfish
1½ to 2 pints *court-bouillon* (page 47)
¼ cup fine light olive oil
2 medium-sized boiled potatoes, peeled, sliced
    ¼-inch thick, the slices then quartered

1 large firm-ripe tomato, skinned, sliced very
   thin
3 hardcooked eggs, sliced
24 pitted ripe olives
1 teaspoon capers, well-drained
1½ teaspoon salt
Generous dash freshly-ground white pepper
4 or 5 thin slices lemon, seeded

Poach the fish in the *court-bouillon,* starting
with the liquid cold. Bring to a boil, and then
reduce heat to a simmer; when simmering
starts, remove from heat and let stand 5 minutes.
Drain the fish, skin, and flake flesh from bones
in large pieces. Heat the oil, put the fish and
potatoes in it to warm, but not to cook. In an
ovenproof dish that can go to the table, combine the fish, potatoes, tomatoes, half the olives,
and all but a half-dozen center slices of the eggs.
Dust the top with salt and pepper, pour over it
any oil remaining in the skillet. Cook covered
in a preheated 225-degree oven for 10 to 15
minutes. Remove from oven, uncover, quickly
dot the top with the reserved egg slices, olives,
capers and lemon slices. This is a meal-sized
salad; serve it with a good Bordeaux-type white
wine (see page 178). Serves 6 to 8.

Although this closes the chapter on panfish,
remember that in later chapters you will find
other recipes suitable for these small nuggets of
goodness. And the reverse is also true; the recipes in this chapter can be used to prepare
other types of fish.

# 5

## CATFISH

If an award was ever to be given to the fish sought by more anglers than any other on the North American continent, the catfish would unquestionably win it, fins down.

Perhaps ubiquity has something to do with it, for catfish swim in virtually every system of waterways the land sustains. They range in size from the giant, coarse-fleshed 200-pounders in the Mississippi River complex to tiny, firm-fleshed toothsome half-pounders in high mountain lakes. Though not exclusively American in origin or habitat, today the catfish is the country's leading freshwater food fish.

Unhappily, the fate of too many catfish is the frying pan. The fish deserves better—or, at least more versatile treatment. Catfish can be cooked by almost any fish recipe. Firm of flesh, easy to clean, almost boneless, the catfish responds nobly to the call of the baking dish, the casserole, the stew pot and the broiler, just as it does to the skillet.

Now, to be practical, the catfish has one peculiarity that makes it different from most other fish: it is skinned rather than scaled, and is cleaned after skinning. To clean a catfish, you need a stout board, a sharp knife, a pair of pliers, and an icepick. Circle the fish's body with a deep cut just behind the gills, and with the tip of your knife work the skin loose from the flesh on the body side of the cut. Pin the fish to the board, belly down, by driving the icepick through its head, then grasp the loosened flap of skin with the pliers and begin pulling it steadily toward the tail. You will have to help your pulling with an occasional touch of the knife point, especially in the fin areas, but if you rely on steady pressure instead of brute strength the skin will peel like a glove being turned inside out. When the tail is reached, cut it off, then slice firmly through the backbone, pull the head down and toward the tail and the insides will all come out.

There are two ways to remove the fins. You can score along the dorsal fin before skinning, and make shallow cuts around the other fins; then, after skinning, cut the fins out of the flesh. Or, to remove fins and skin at the same time, insert the tip of your knife at the back of the dorsal fin to a depth of about ½ inch and make slanting cuts on both sides of the fin in the direction of the head. Leave about half the fin attached to the skin. Make similar undercuts at the back of each of the other fins, and when the skin is pulled away the fins will pull free at the same time.

With the help of the following recipes, the rest is up to you.

## Fried Catfish, with Hushpuppies

This is the dish most commonly associated with catfish. Because it is generally served to a crowd, no quantities are given; you can adjust the quantity needed to serve your group by remembering that a half-pound of fish should be allowed per person, and that one cup of cornmeal will coat about three pounds of fish pieces. You will need:

## How to Clean a Catfish

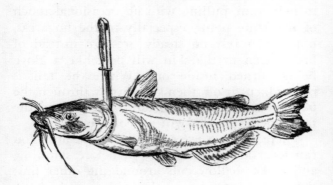

First, girdle the body with a sharp knife just behind the gills. With the tip of the blade, work the skin loose from the flesh.

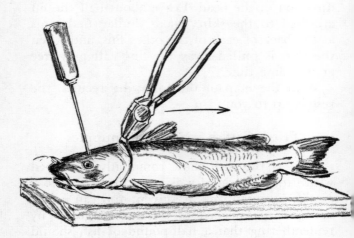

Pin fish to board with an icepick. Then use pliers to pull skin toward tail. When you reach the tail cut it off.

Cut through the backbone and bend head down.

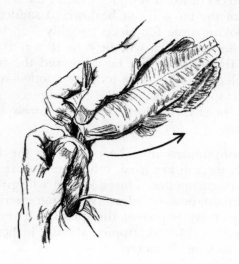

Pull head down and toward the tail. The insides will come out. Then remove the fins as described in the text.

**Catfish, skinned and cleaned, cut in fairly uniform pieces**
**Cornmeal**
**Salt; allow ½ teaspoon per cup of cornmeal**
**Pepper; a generous dash per cup of cornmeal**
**Fat in a big kettle for deep frying; obviously, the size of the kettle determines the quantity of fat required; the level should be maintained at about ¾ full**

Have the fat in the kettle just under smoking-hot—on a cooking thermometer, between 370 and 380 degrees. Mix the cornmeal, salt and pepper together, wipe the pieces of catfish with a damp cloth and roll them in the seasoned cornmeal. Do not overload the kettle; put in the pieces of fish a few at a time so the temperature of the fat will not be lowered suddenly.

Cooking time for pieces roughly 3 inches by 2 inches by 1 inch will be 8 to 10 minutes; by then the outsides will be crisp, and the insides completely cooked. Use tongs or a long-handled, slotted spoon to fish out the cooked pieces; drain them briefly on cloth or paper towels before serving.

Hushpuppies *must* be cooked in the fat in which the fish are fried, otherwise they're nothing but cornpones. The following will give you a hint on how to adjust your ingredients for the quantity required; the quantity given produces 12 to 14 hushpuppies, about 2 inches long by 1 inch in diameter:

**2 cups white cornmeal**
**½ teaspoon salt**
**½ to ¾ cup boiling water**

Stir the ingredients into a thick dough and form the hushpuppies in your hands to make small rounded pones. Drop them into the hot fat a few at a time, and cook for 5 to 8 minutes; strain out with a slotted spoon when nicely brown, or remove with tongs. Drain on cloth or paper towels for a few moments.

## Baked Poached Catfish

4 to 5-pound catfish, skinned and cleaned
1½ quarts cold water
1 tablespoon salt
1 tablespoon tarragon vinegar
½ teaspoon cracked or knife-nicked peppercorns
2 bay leaves
4 or 5 pieces green celery tops with leaves
3 or 4 sprigs fresh parsley
2 whole cloves
1 clove garlic
3 to 4 tablespoons Anchovy Butter (page 171)
½ to ¾ cup fine dry breadcrumbs

Put the fish in a deep kettle or fish poacher; if it does not rest on a rack, wrap in cheesecloth so it can be removed without breaking when cooked. Pour in the water and add all other ingredients except Anchovy Butter and breadcrumbs. Bring to a boil, then reduce to a simmer; cook 5 minutes after simmering starts, remove the pan from heat and let the fish stay in the liquid until it cools. (If desired, the fish can be poached in advance and kept refrigerated until time to be baked.) Remove fish from liquid, drain well, wipe dry, then divide into two halves (page 38) and remove backbone and rib bones. Rub the pieces generously with Anchovy Butter, coating all sides. Lay on a buttered, ovenproof platter; if you wish, reconstitute the fish by arranging the two halves one atop the other. Cook in a preheated 325-degree oven for 15 minutes, sprinkle with breadcrumbs, put under the broiler for 3 or 4 minutes until the breadcrumbs brown. Serves 4 to 6.

## Baked Stuffed Catfish, Creole Style

3- to 4-pound catfish, skinned and cleaned
4 cups large coarse crumbs of good French bread
½ teaspoon crumbled or powdered basil
½ teaspoon crumbled or powdered thyme
1 teaspoon salt
Large dash freshly-ground white pepper
1 egg, lightly beaten
1 cup diced salt pork or fat bacon, browned in skillet and drained
4 large, red-ripe, fresh tomatoes or 2 cups canned tomatoes
1 teaspoon salt
½ teaspoon pepper
1 teaspoon cider or grain vinegar
1 medium-sized sweet onion, peeled and sliced
½ small green (Bell) pepper, cleaned and coarsely diced
3 slices blanched salt pork or fat bacon

If you feel like taking on the job, remove the backbone and biggest ribs from the fish, working through the cavity; also remove the dorsal spines. This does not affect the dish in any way, but makes serving easier.

Combine breadcrumbs, basil, thyme, salt, pepper, egg, and pork dice. Stuff the cavity of the fish, spreading it wide; reserve any remaining stuffing. Butter a baking dish and put the stuffed fish on it, belly down. Mix the tomatoes, salt, pepper, vinegar, onion and green pepper and pour this over the stuffed fish. Scatter the remaining stuffing on the surface of the dressing, but none on the back of the fish. Blanch the salt pork or bacon by plunging into boiling water 3 to 4 minutes; lay these over the back of the fish. Bake uncovered in a preheated 350-degree oven for 35 minutes; spoon some of the pan liquid over the back of the fish once or twice. Ten minutes before removing from oven, slip the pork slices off the top of the fish and into the pan juices. Serves 6.

## Catfish au Gratin

- **3- to 4-pound catfish, skinned and cleaned**
- **2 cups fish stock (page 46)**
- **1 tablespoon butter or margarine**
- **3 cups Sauce Mornay (page 167)**
- **2 to 3 tablespoons grated Parmesan cheese**

Poach the fish in the stock, allowing 15 minutes cooking time after bringing the liquid to a boil; then reduce to a simmer. Drain, remove bones, and cut flesh into cubes of about

¾ inch. Butter a shallow baking dish or small individual gratin dishes and put the pieces of fish into it (or them). Add enough Sauce Mornay to cover the fish pieces about ⅔ of the way up their sides. Sprinkle generously with Parmesan, put under the broiler 3 to 4 minutes, until the sauce is bubbling furiously and the cheese topping is a rich brown. (If you wish, circle the baking dishes with a border of Duchess Potatoes before putting in the fish and sauce; if you do this, brush the potatoes with egg white so they will brown evenly and take on a nice crisp crust.) Serves 4 to 6.

## Catfish in Sour Cream

3- to 4-pound catfish, skinned and cleaned
½ cup flour (approximately)
⅓ cup butter or solid margarine
½ pound fresh mushrooms
1 cup light cream or evaporated milk, diluted 2½ parts milk to 1 part water
¾ cup dairy sour cream
½ teaspoon meat extract: BV, Bovril, etc.
½ teaspoon salt
Large pinch freshly-ground white pepper
Small pinch nutmeg
1 teaspoon paprika
¾ to 1 cup fine dry breadcrumbs

Cut the fish into strips about 1½ to 2 inches long by ½ inch thick and wide. Remove bones while doing this. Roll the strips in flour. Slice the mushrooms about ¼ inch thick. Sauté the mushrooms in the butter over moderate heat about 1 minute per side; add the pieces of fish and cook 3 to 4 minutes, turning to brown them evenly. The pieces of catfish should be a healthy but light golden tan. Over very low heat combine the cream, sour cream, meat extract, salt, pepper and nutmeg. Scrape into this liquid the fish, mushrooms, and any pan juices. Stir well, and then pour into a shallow gratin dish or individual gratin dishes. Combine the paprika and breadcrumbs and sprinkle the top of the dish or dishes generously. Cook for 10 to 12 minutes in a pre-heated 325-degree oven and finish under the broiler if necessary to brown the topping to a rich, deep color. Serves 4 generously, 6 in a pinch.

## Catfish Sicilian Style

3- to 4-pound catfish, skinned and cleaned
½ cup milk or evaporated milk diluted with equal parts water
¼ cup flour
¼ cup olive oil
1 tablespoon minced fresh parsley
1 clove garlic, minced or mashed
½ cup white wine vinegar
¼ cup fish stock (page 46)
4 large ripe tomatoes, peeled and seeded, with all juices reserved, cut in coarse chunks
1 teaspoon salt
Large dash freshly-ground white pepper

Cut the catfish into slices 1 to 1½ inches thick, cutting across the body at right angles. Dip the slices in milk and roll in flour. Wipe off any excess flour; a thin coating is all that's required. Heat the oil in a heavy skillet, and sauté the fish slices 3 minutes per side; they should be a rich brown. Combine all remaining ingredients and pour over the fish in the skillet. Cover and cook 15 to 20 minutes over medium heat. Serve with thick slices of generously-buttered Italian bread. Serves 4 to 6.

## Catfish in Sherry Sauce

3- to 4-pound catfish, skinned and cleaned
2 tablespoons lemon juice
¼ cup butter (no substitutes)
2 tablespoons minced shallots
1 tablespoon grated sweet onion
½ cup fish stock (page 46)
¾ cup medium-dry Sherry (see page 178)
2 egg yolks
¾ cup heavy cream or undiluted evaporated milk
½ teaspoon salt
Small dash freshly-ground white pepper

Divide the fish lengthwise, cutting along the back to the backbone and removing the dorsal spines, backbone and large ribs (see page 11). Rub the halves with lemon juice, and reserve any remaining juice. Melt the butter in a shallow baking dish and sauté the shallots and onions until they just begin to soften; do not allow them to brown. Combine the remaining lemon juice with the fish stock and sherry and pour into the pan. When it begins to simmer, put the two pieces of fish in the pan, cover and cook in a preheated 400-degree oven for 15 minutes. Beat the egg yolks lightly, combine them with the cream, salt and pepper, and bring them to the boiling point. Then pour over the fish pieces in the pan, and cook uncovered for another 10 minutes, reducing the oven temperature to 325 degrees. Serves 4 to 6.

## Catfish with Vermouth

- 4- to 5-pound catfish, skinned and cleaned, or equivalent weight in smaller fish
- 1 teaspoon salt
- ¼ teaspoon freshly-ground white pepper
- ½ cup butter or solid margarine
- ½ cup dry Vermouth
- ¼ cup fish stock (page 46)
- 4 or 5 drops Peychaud Bitters
- ¾ to 1 cup fine dry breadcrumbs
- ⅓ cup grated Parmesan cheese

Cut the fish into slices 1 inch thick, and dust lightly with salt and pepper. Use about ½ to ¾ teaspoon of the butter to grease a shallow baking dish. Arrange the slices of fish on the bottom of the dish. Over very low heat, combine the butter with the Vermouth, fish stock and bitters. (If your taste calls for Angostura Bitters, feel free to substitute.) Pour this liquid over the fish slices. Cook uncovered in a preheated 350-degree oven for 20 minutes, basting two or three times with the pan juices. Combine the breadcrumbs and cheese, sprinkle over the fish slices, and finish under the broiler for 2 or three minutes, until nicely browned. Serves 4 to 6.

## Catfish Hash

2 cups raw catfish cut into ½-inch cubes, bones removed

2 cups raw potatoes cut into ½-inch cubes

1 medium-sized sweet onion diced coarsely

2 slices blanched salt pork, ½-inch thick, diced

¼ cup thick cream or undiluted evaporated milk

1 teaspoon salt

¼ teaspoon pepper

Put the catfish, potatoes, and onions in a saucepan, cover with boiling water, and cook for 15 minutes at a brisk simmer. Drain well through a sieve or colander. Blanch the pork by plunging it into boiling water for 3 to 4 minutes, then dice and sauté until very crisp. Strain the pork from the pan. Mash the catfish-potato-onion mixture, and then combine with the pork dice. Beat in the cream and seasonings. Pour off the pork fat from the skillet, leaving only the fat that clings to the bottom. Bring the pan to medium heat. Form the hash into one large, pan-sized patty or into small individual patties and sauté until crisply browned on both sides. Serves 6.

## Catfish Pudding

3 pound center cut from a large catfish

1½ teaspoons salt

4 large boiled potatoes, peeled and sliced ¼ inch

¼ teaspoon freshly-ground white pepper
¼ teaspoon nutmeg
½ teaspoon crumbled thyme
4 eggs
4 cups very cold milk
¼ cup melted butter
¾ cup fine fresh breadcrumbs

Slice the fish at right angles to the body in ¼-inch slices, removing bones. Rub each slice on both sides with salt and lay on a cloth-covered dish; put a layer of cloth between slices if they are stacked. Spread a cloth over the top layer of fish slices and put a second plate on top. Refrigerate the weighted slices at least 6 hours. Butter a casserole dish that can be used as a serving dish. Cover the bottom with a layer of potato slices, then a layer of fish slices, dusting the fish slices with the pepper, nutmeg and thyme. Build up the dish with alternate layers of potato and fish slices, dusting each layer of fish slices with the seasonings. Top with a layer of potatoes. Beat the eggs lightly, add the milk slowly while beating, and also beat in ½ cup of the breadcrumbs, adding them by tablespoonsful. When the milk and breadcrumbs have all been blended with the eggs, quickly beat in the melted butter and pour this over the layers in the casserole. Sprinkle the top with the remaining breadcrumbs. Cook uncovered in a preheated 325-degree oven for 35 to 40 minutes, or until the eggs set up into a custard. Serve with a white sauce, such as Velouté or Suprême (see pages 168 and 169), or with melted butter, passed separately. This pudding

is also very good served cold. To prepare for
cold service, line the baking dish with foil, butter the foil, build up the dish as described, and
cook. Cool, then chill in the refrigerator for
2 hours or longer. Turn out on a plate, strip
away the foil, and slice like a cake. Plain mayonnaise or one of the white sauces lightly
chilled is good with the cold pudding. Serves
6 to 8.

Don't end your catfish cookery with the dozen
recipes in this chapter, thinking that they're
the only ones suitable. Even though other recipes aren't tagged specifically for catfish, most
of them can be used for this pleasant fellow. As
a suggestion, try a Matelote of Catfish, using
the recipes on page 156 and 157, or take thin
slices off a big one and cook them à la Meunière,
as given on page 95, or cook thick cross-cut
steaks off a big fish in the style suggested for
salmon steaks on page 123. And this is just a
start—there are many other methods of cooking
what in all fairness must be called the All-
American fish.

# C

## BLACK BASS

If the catfish is entitled to be called the All-American food fish, the black bass has certainly earned the honor of being designated the All-American game fish. Smallmouth or large, the *Micropterus* is the prime target of anglers who fish for sport first and food second.

Whether an angler's pleasure is a placid Southern pond, where husky-shouldered large-mouths lurk amid brush under the lily-pads, or a fast-moving river where hard-hitting small-mouths hang behind the rocks, the black bass rewards whoever hooks him with a battle. Black bass also earn high marks as tasty fish to grace a table, and those who complain that the flesh of bass is dry and pallid and tastes of moss simply have not learned how to cook and clean them properly.

There is a small secret connected with the cleaning of black bass, especially big lunkers from warm southern waters. Cut away the skin for a half-inch or so around each fin and remove the fins themselves with deep circling cuts that go to their root muscles. It is in the areas around the fins that algae find lodging, and scrubbing or scraping cannot remove them. These algae are what give black bass the "mossy" taste.

As for cooking bass, the fish has an unusually delicate flavor that needs herbs and seasonings with which it can blend harmoniously. Skillet cooking and simple seasoning should be reserved for bass weighing less than a pound;

bigger bass need poaching in stock or *court-bouillon,* or baking with liquids and herbal bouquets that give their flesh a tastebud-pleasing savor. Big bass can be sautéed, but when cooked this way the fat in the pan should be pre-flavored; or, serve an assertive sauce with the fish. The angler-chef who observes these simple precepts will be rewarded with as much pleasure when eating black bass as he got when catching them.

## Black Bass with Walnuts

2½- to 3-pound bass
2 cups fish stock (page 46)
1 tablespoon butter or solid margarine
¾ cup coarsely chopped or broken walnut meats
1 cup dairy sour cream
⅓ cup lemon juice
Stingy pinch grated horseradish
Small pinch of salt

After cleaning and scaling the fish, remove head and tail; cut out fins and the skin surrounding them. Wrap fish loosely in cheesecloth (the cheesecloth wrapping is only for easy removal of the fish from the poaching liquid; it can be omitted if a poaching pan is used) and poach in the stock by bringing to a boil, then reducing to a simmer. Cooking time will be 20 to 25 minutes after the simmering begins. Drain fish from stock, transfer to a warmed platter, and slip off skin. If you feel like making the extra effort, divide the fish into two pieces by the method given on page 38. Melt the butter over low heat and sauté the walnut meats until crisp but not brown. Combine the sour cream, lemon juice, horseradish and salt with ½ cup of the hot stock in which the bass was poached. Pour this into the pan with the walnut meats and cook 3 to 4 minutes, just long enough to marry the flavors, before pouring it over the skinned fish on its platter. Serves 4 to 6.

## Bass in Beer

- 3- to 4-pound black bass
- 3 tablespoons butter or solid margarine
- 1½ tablespoons flour
- 2½ cups beer, at room temperature
- 1 teaspoon salt
- ¾ teaspoon brown sugar
- 3 or 4 peppercorns, cracked or nicked with a knife
- ½ teaspoon nutmeg
- 1 tablespoon lemon juice

Clean and scale the bass; remove the head, tail, fins and the skin around them, and divide the fish into slices about 1½ inches thick, cutting at right angles to the body. Melt butter in a deep skillet over moderate heat, slowly add the flour while stirring until a smooth paste is formed. Cook for 3 to 4 minutes without allowing the paste to brown. Pour in the beer in a slow, steady stream while stirring briskly with a slotted spoon or whisk to keep lumps from forming. Put in the seasonings, and then add the fish slices. Cover the pan and cook over low heat, the liquid just bubbling gently, for 5 minutes; turn the fish slices, and cook 5 minutes more. Drain the fish slices from the sauce, letting the liquid return to the pan. Put the slices on a warmed platter or individual service plates, slip off the skin, and remove bones. Increase heat under the sauce until it thickens to the consistency of a heavy cream, then strain over the fish. Serve with hot boiled potatoes or thick slices of unbuttered toast for dunking in the sauce. Serves 4 to 6.

## Black Bass Italian Style

4 bass, ¾ to 1 pound each
1 to 1½ teaspoon salt
¾ to 1 teaspoon freshly-ground white pepper
3 tablespoons olive oil (If you don't enjoy the flavor of olive oil, substitute clarified butter, page 32)
3 tablespoons minced sweet onion
1 clove garlic, threaded on a string
1 cup fish stock (page 46)
½ cup tomato paste
1 teaspoon minced fresh basil or 1½ teaspoons crumbled dry or powdered basil

Clean and scale the bass, remove heads, tails, fins and the skin around them. Rub the fish lightly inside and out with salt and pepper and sauté in the oil over moderate heat, cooking 5 to 7 minutes per side, depending upon their size. Remove the fish to a heated service platter or individual plates. Sauté the onion and garlic in the fat remaining in the pan; when the onion is a deep gold in color, fish out the garlic by its string and add the fish stock, tomato paste and basil to the onions in the pan. Stir occasionally while this simmers 4 to 5 minutes; then pour over the fish. Hot buttered Italian bread or hard rolls go well with this. Serves 4.

## Black Bass Plantation Style

4 bass, ¾ to 1 pound each
1½ cups cooked white rice
½ cup grated Parmesan cheese
½ cup grated mild cheese, Longhorn or
   Gruyere
½ teaspoon salt
¼ teaspoon cayenne or ⅛ teaspoon Nepal
   pepper
1 egg
4 tablespoons butter or solid margarine
1 to 2 tablespoons flour

Clean and scale the bass, remove fins and the skin around them, trim tails, but leave heads on the fish. Pound the rice, cold and dry, into a crumbly paste; combine it with the two cheeses, salt and pepper. Beat the egg lightly and stir into the rice mixture. Stuff the fish with this, closing the openings with small skewers or by sewing. Rub the outsides of the fish very lightly with butter and roll in flour; shake off any clots of flour that form. Melt the remaining butter in a heavy skillet with a tightly-fitting lid and sauté the fish over low to moderate heat with the pan closed. Cook gently, 7 to 8 minutes per side. The New Orleans Sauce, page 176, goes well with bass cooked in this fashion. Serves 4.

## Black Bass with White Grapes

4 small bass, ½ to ¾ pound each
3 tablespoons flour
1 teaspoon salt
¼ teaspoon freshly-ground white pepper
¼ pound butter (no substitutes)
¾ cup Rhine-type white wine (see page 178)
1 cup seedless white grapes
3 tablespoons brandy—a cognac is preferred

Clean and scale the fish, remove fins and the skin around them; trim tails, but leave the heads on. Toss the flour, salt and pepper together in a plastic bag and rub a light, even coating of the seasoned flour over the fish; it may be necessary to wipe them first with a damp cloth to make the coating stick properly. Sauté the fish gently in the butter over low to moderate heat, cooking 4 to 5 minutes per side, depending upon size. Pour the wine into the pan with the fish, and when it begins to bubble and simmer, remove pan from heat, cover it, and let it stand 5 minutes. Drain the bass from the pan, letting the liquid flow back into it; put the fish on a warmed platter or individual service plates. Skin the bass at this point, if you feel like it. Over brisk heat, bring the pan liquid to a boil and cook until it is reduced to half its volume. Put the grapes in a heatproof dish, warm the brandy, pour it over the grapes and ignite it; when the flames die, put the grapes into the pan, scraping the dish to get off all brandy essence. Stir the pan juices once or twice and pour over the fish. Serves 4 delightfully.

# Black Bass Philadelphia Style
## (sometimes called Maryland Style)

5-pound bass, or two or three smaller fish
1 to 1½ teaspoons salt
¾ to 1 teaspoon freshly-ground white pepper
⅛ pound butter (no substitutes)
1 tablespoon chopped shallots
½ cup rye whiskey (or Irish whiskey)
1½ cups heavy cream or undiluted evaporated milk
2 egg yolks
⅓ cup dry Sherry (see page 178)

If you are using a single large fish, cut it into quarters and skin it; if several small fish, cut them in halves or thirds, depending upon size, and remove skin. Dust the pieces well with salt and pepper. Melt the butter in a heavy, deep skillet or saucepan with a tightly-fitting cover. Put in the shallots and pieces of fish and cook covered, turning the fish so the pieces will cook 3 to 4 minutes per side. Set aside 3 tablespoons of the whiskey; warm the remainder, pour over the fish in the pan and ignite. When the flames die down, pour in 1 cup of cream, cover the pan, and cook at very low heat for 5 to 7 minutes, depending upon the size of the fish pieces. When the fish flakes readily, drain the pieces out with a slotted spoon, letting the juices flow back into the pan; put the pieces of fish on a warmed platter. Beat the egg yolk with the remaining cream, whiskey, and Sherry. Pour into the pan and cook 5 minutes without boiling. Strain the sauce over the fish. Serve with plain boiled rice. Serves 6.

## Black Bass Bourguinonne

3½ to 4-pound bass
1 teaspoon salt
Large pinch freshly-ground white pepper
4 tablespoons butter (no substitutes)
1 teaspoon sugar
24 small white boiling onions, ¾ to 1 inch in diameter
12 to 16 small button mushrooms, fresh or canned
3 cups dry red Burgundy-type wine (see page 178)
1 teaspoon meat extract; BV, Bovril, etc.

Clean and scale the fish, remove head, trim tail, and cut out fins and the skin around them. Rub the cavity with salt and pepper, and rub the seasonings well into the raw flesh where the head and fins have been cut off. Let the fish rest 10 to 15 minutes after putting on the seasonings. Melt ¾ tablespoon butter in a saucepan, add the sugar, and over medium-high heat sauté the onions, rolling them around until they turn an even, golden brown. Sauté fresh mushrooms separately in just enough butter to put a film on the pan, and cook for 2 to 3 minutes; if canned mushrooms are used, no cooking is necessary. Butter a shallow ovenproof baking dish and put the bass in it. Strew the onions and mushrooms over the fish, and pour the wine in. Cook uncovered in a preheated 275-degree oven for 40 minutes, basting the fish occasionally with wine from the pan. Lift the fish out carefully without breaking it and slip off its skin before putting it on a warmed platter. Drain the onions and mushrooms from the pan; arrange them around the fish. On top of the stove, over high heat, boil the pan juice until it is reduced to half its volume. Stir in the remaining butter and the meat extract to form a smooth, creamy sauce. Taste and adjust seasoning; a tiny pinch of salt may be required, depending on the kind of meat extract used. Pour the sauce over the fish and carry it proudly to the table. Serves 4 to 6.

## Baked Black Bass

3½- to 4-pound bass
⅓ cup lemon juice
¼ pound butter or solid margarine
2 egg yolks, lightly beaten
1 teaspoon capers
½ teaspoon dillseed
1½ teaspoons cider vinegar
½ teaspoon salt

Clean and scale fish, remove head, trim tail, and cut out fins and the skin around them. Brush the cavity well with lemon juice; also brush the raw flesh where the head and fins were removed. With a sharp-tined fork, pierce the thickest sections of the fish and let a little of the lemon juice trickle in while angling the fork to hold the holes open. Do this on both sides; then, let the fish rest about 10 minutes before cooking. Bake on a fine-meshed rack or a slotted or perforated broiler pan in a preheated 375-degree oven for 35 to 40 minutes. Baste occasionally with the remaining lemon juice creamed into 1 teaspoon butter. While the fish is cooking: Cream the remaining butter with the egg yolks and blend into this the capers, dillseed, vinegar and salt. Have a warmed ovenproof platter ready. Take the fish from the oven, slip the skin off the top side, and then divide according to method given on page 38. Transfer the first half to the platter, placing it with the inner side up, and spread with half the butter mixture; put the other half on top, inner side down, and spread with the remainder of the butter mixture. If the fish breaks during its transfer from broiler rack to platter, re-form it on the platter. Return to the oven for 10 minutes and then serve by cutting slices at right angles to the body. Serves 4 to 6.

## Baked Stuffed Black Bass

4- to 5-pound bass
4 or 5 anchovy fillets, drained and wiped dry
2 paper-thin slices of lemon, seeded
1 to 1½ cups coarse dry breadcrumbs
1 teaspoon salt
Large dash freshly-ground white pepper
2 to 3 tablespoons dry white Burgundy-type wine (see page 178)
1 egg, lightly beaten
1 tablespoon butter or solid margarine
1 teaspoon lemon juice
1 cup Sauce Velouté (page 168)
1 tablespoon minced fresh parsley

Clean and scale the fish; leave the head on, but trim tail, cut out fins and the skin around them. Mince the anchovy fillets and lemon slices and combine them with the breadcrumbs and seasonings; moisten with the wine and stir in the beaten egg. Stuff the cavity of the fish, closing it with small skewers or with a few stitches. Bake in a shallow, buttered pan in a preheated 375-degree oven for 35 to 40 minutes, depending upon the size of the fish. Cream together the butter and lemon juice, and baste the fish several times during cooking. Remove fish to a heated platter and slip off the skin. Warm the Sauce Velouté and pour over the fish; sprinkle with minced parsley. Serves 6.

## Baked Bass with Rosemary

3- to 4-pound bass
¾ teaspoon salt
Scanty dash of freshly-ground white pepper
¼ cup butter or solid margarine
½ cup grated sweet onion
½ clove garlic, minced or mashed
½ cup fish stock (page 46)
2 tablespoons lemon juice
2 teaspoons grated lemon rind
1½ teaspoons fresh rosemary, minced, or 2
    teaspoons dried rosemary, crumbled

Clean and scale the fish; remove head and tail, and cut out fins and the skin around them. Dust the fish very lightly with salt and pepper. Melt butter in a shallow, heatproof dish and in it sauté the onion and garlic; when the onion begins to become transparent, lay the bass on the onion in the pan. Combine the fish stock, lemon juice and rind, and the rosemary; pour over the bass. Cover the dish and cook in a preheated 350-degree oven for 35 to 40 minutes, depending upon size of the fish. Serves 4 to 6.

## Black Bass Lisbon Style

4 small bass, ¾ to 1 pound each
1½ teaspoons olive oil (drawn butter, page 32, can be substituted if you do not like the flavor of olive oil)
2 tablespoons chopped sweet onion
4 large ripe tomatoes, peeled and seeded, juices drained, chopped coarsely (substitute equivalent quantity of canned tomatoes if fresh ones not available)
1 clove garlic, minced or crushed
1 tablespoon coarsely-chopped fresh parsley
¼ teaspoon powdered marjoram
½ bay leaf, tied to a long thread
½ teaspoon salt
¾ cup dry red wine; best choice is a California Zinfandel (see page 178)
½ cup light cream or evaporated milk diluted 2½ parts milk to 1 part water
1 tablespoon butter or solid margarine
1 tablespoon flour

Clean and scale fish, cut them into 3 or 4 pieces of approximately equal size, discarding heads, tails, fins and the skin around the fins. Heat the oil in a heavy skillet that can go to the oven, and sauté the onion, tomatoes, garlic, parsley and rosemary very gently for 5 or 6 minutes. Bury the bay leaf in the vegetables, and put the bass pieces on top of them. Combine the wine and cream and pour into the pan. Cover pan and cook in a preheated 325-degree oven for 20 minutes. Lift out the fish, putting it on a warmed platter; drain the vegetables from the pan with a slotted spoon, letting the juices flow back into the pan. Remove and discard bay leaf; arrange the vegetables around the pieces of fish on the platter. Bring the juices in the pan to a gentle simmer. Knead butter and flour into a smooth paste and flake into the pan, stirring until each addition dissolves, and letting the juices simmer at least 5 minutes after the last bit of the paste has been added. Pour the sauce over the fish pieces and serve with generous slices of fresh, crusty bread. Serves 4 to 6.

## Bass with Celery Stuffing

3½ to 4-pound bass
¾ teaspoon salt
Pinch of freshly-ground white pepper
3 tablespoons butter or solid margarine
2 tablespoons grated sweet onion
½ cup celeriac (celery root, sometimes called celery knob) peeled, slice paper-thin, and shredded into slivers the thickness of toothpicks
3 sprigs of fresh green celery tops with leaves
1 to 1½ cups coarse fresh breadcrumbs
Juice of 1 fresh lime or 1½ tablespoons bottled lime juice
3 tablespoons butter or solid margarine
¼ teaspoon grated Sapsago cheese

Clean and scale the fish, trim tail, and remove fins and the skin around them; leave the head on. Dust fish sparingly inside and out with salt and pepper. In 3 tablespoons butter, sauté the onion and celeriac until the onion begins to become transparent; add the sprigs of celery tops to the pan when you begin to cook this, but remove them before adding other ingredients. When the onions begin to clear, remove the pan from heat, stir in the breadcrumbs and lime juice, and use this to stuff the cavity of the fish. Close the cavity with small skewers or by sewing. Using about 1 tablespoon butter, grease a shallow baking pan and put the fish in it. Cook uncovered in a pre-heated 375-degree oven for 35 to 45 minutes, depending upon size of fish. Combine the remaining butter with the Sapsago cheese and brush the fish with the mixture three or four times as it cooks. Serves 4 to 6.

## Bass Branca

- 2 bass of about 2 pounds each
- 2 leeks
- 1 heart of celery, with leaves
- 1 sweet red pepper, cleaned and seeded, cut in ¼-inch strips
- ½ teaspoon salt
- 3 tablespoons olive oil or drawn butter (page 32)
- 1 cup mushrooms, sliced about ⅛ inch
- ½ cup grated sweet onion
- ½ clove garlic, minced or mashed
- 6 red-ripe tomatoes, skinned and seeded, or equivalent in well-drained canned tomatoes
- 2 sprigs fresh parsley
- 1 teaspoon powdered marjoram
- 1 bay leaf, on a long thread
- 1 cup dry white Bordeaux-type wine (see page 178)

½ teaspoon lemon juice
2 tablespoons chopped fresh parsley

Clean and scale the bass; cut them into 1-inch slices, cutting at right angles to the body, and discard head, tail, fins and the skin around the fins. Trim the roots and green tops off the leeks, sliver them and the celery heart into match-stick-sized pieces, combine them with the red pepper, sprinkle with salt, and sauté in 1 table-spoon oil over very low heat until they just begin to soften; do not let them get brown or turn mushy. In a separate pan, sauté the onion and garlic in 1 tablespoon oil until the onion softens; then add the tomatoes, parsley, mar-joram and bay leaf. Cook until the tomatoes can be pulped easily. Remove parsley and bay leaf, combine the leek-celery-pepper mixture with the onion-tomato mixture, and spread half of it on the bottom of a buttered baking dish. Put the fish on this and cover with the remain-ing vegetable mixture. Combine the wine and lemon juice and pour into the pan. Cook un-covered in a preheated 350-degree oven for 45 minutes. Sprinkle chopped parsley over the top of the dish before taking it to the table. Serves 4 to 6.

This doesn't close the book on bass, of course. Look further, and you'll find recipes for the Bourride, page 96, one for a Spanish-style fish stew on page 112, to say nothing of the Louisiana dish on page 145. So, when you have black bass to cook, don't stop after exhausting this one chapter. Look among other pages to find new ways of cooking our country's top sport fish.

# 7

# PIKE, PICKEREL, MUSKELLUNGE

Until bombarded by the debris we tossed into their homes, the pike family was king of the rivers and a wide spread of lakes and ponds as well. Today, in the clean waters they seek, both by choice and necessity, the pike family still reigns unchallenged. Any fisherman who has ever sought them knows of their cunning ways in avoiding even the most tempting lures. And no angler-chef who has ever cooked them consistently can keep from boasting about the sweetness of their flesh.

There's no mistaking the members of the *Esox* clan; they are long and lean of jaw and body, swift predators and stubborn fighters. They have been given numerous names, but whether you call them dory, jack, snake, sauger, redfin or sandpikes, if you give them proper treatment in the kitchen, they will respond by giving you enjoyment at the table.

Because the lean bodies of all members of the family conceal a complex, bony inner structure, pike, pickerel and muskies are generally poached whole or in sections, filleted, stuffed or baked. Needless to say, any recipe suitable for one member of the family will serve to guide you in preparing a cousin. And though the walleye, often mistakenly considered a member of the pike family, is actually a second cousin two or three times removed, any recipe suitable for pike is also good for walleye.

## Pike Fillets au Gratin

4 large pike fillets
½ teaspoon salt
Generous dash freshly-ground white pepper
2½ tablespoons butter or solid margarine
1½ cups light cream or evaporated milk diluted 2½ parts milk to 1 part water
1 egg
¾ cup grated, medium-sharp cheddar cheese (real cheese, not "process cheese food")
½ teaspoon grated Sapsago cheese


Dust the fillets very lightly with salt and pepper and sauté them over moderate heat, using 1½ tablespoons of butter and cooking 2 minutes per side. Transfer the fillets to a buttered gratin dish or to individual gratin dishes. Beat the egg lightly, combine it with the cream, melt the remaining butter with what is left in the pan from cooking the fillets, and stir the melted butter into the egg-cream mixture. Pour this over the fillets and sprinkle the mixed cheddar and Sapsago cheese over the top. Cook in a preheated 400-degree oven 5 to 6 minutes; if the cheese topping has not browned by that time, put under the broiler for a moment until it becomes a deep tan. Serves 4.

## Pike Fillets, Brugge Style

4 large pike fillets
¾ head of curly endive (in some areas this
    leaf vegetable is called chicory)
2 tablespoons chopped shallots
½ cup cream or evaporated milk diluted 3
    parts milk to 1 part water
¾ cup Rhine-type white wine (see page 178)
4 thin slices lemon, seeded
2 tablespoons butter (no substitutes)
Scanty pinch of salt
Small dash of freshly-ground white pepper

Blot the fillets dry. Butter a shallow baking
dish and cover the bottom thickly—at least 1
inch deep—with the choice green, leafy portions
of endive, discarding the white stalks and center sections of the leaves. Scatter the shallots
over the endive and lay the fillets on this green
nest. Combine the cream and wine and pour
over the fillets. Cover the pan and cook in a
preheated 350-degree oven for 12 to 15 minutes,
depending upon the thickness of the fillets.
Once or twice while cooking, uncover the pan
long enough to baste the fillets lightly with the
pan liquid. Place a lemon slice on each fillet
and with the pan uncovered, cook 5 minutes
longer. Remove each fillet with the endive beneath it to a warmed service plate, letting the
pan liquids drain back into the pan. On top
of the stove, over brisk heat, bring the liquid
to a seething boil, stir in salt and pepper, taste,
and adjust seasoning; avoid over-salting. Divide
the sauce over the portions and serve. Serves 4.

# Poached Pike with Butter Sauce

4- to 5-pound pike
1½ quarts *court-bouillon* (page 47)
2 tablespoons chopped shallots
¾ cup white wine vinegar
1½ pounds butter (no substitutes)
½ teaspoon salt
Large dash freshly-ground white pepper


Poach the pike in the *court-bouillon*, bringing the liquid to a boil and then reducing the
heat until it simmers very gently. Cook 20 to
25 minutes from the time simmering begins,
depending upon the size of the fish. Drain the
pike well, remove to a warm platter, slip its
skin off, and flake its flesh from the bones in
large pieces. Over brisk heat, boil 1 tablespoon
of the shallots in the vinegar until the liquid
is reduced to half its volume; stir to keep the
shallots from scorching. Strain the reduced
vinegar into a clean saucepan. Cut 1 pound of
butter into small chunks and melt it in the
vinegar over very low heat. As soon as the butter has been placed in the pan, begin beating
it with a wooden spoon and continue beating
as it melts. As soon as the butter starts melting,
add the remaining shallots. Beat until the butter and vinegar combine into a creamy, frothy
sauce; then cut the remaining butter into small
pieces and beat into the sauce to smooth and
refine its texture. Spread the sauce over the
pieces of pike and serve at once with crusty
hard rolls or French bread. Serves 4 generously,
6 adequately.

## Pike Fillets Ambassador

4 large pike fillets
Stingy pinch of salt
Sparse dash of freshly-ground white pepper
1 tablespoon butter (no substitutes)
1 tablespoon finely-minced shallots
1 tablespoon finely-minced fresh parsley
3 tablespoons lemon juice
¾ cup fish stock (page 46)
¾ cup dry, white Burgundy-type wine (see page 178)
1½ cups heavy cream or undiluted evaporated milk
2 egg yolks

Dust the fillets very lightly with salt and pepper and place them in a baking dish that has a bare film of butter on its bottom. Combine the butter, shallots, parsley and lemon juice and spread a portion over the top of each fillet. Stir together the fish stock and wine and pour into the pan; it should barely cover the fillets. Cook covered in a preheated 350-degree oven for 12 to 14 minutes. Remove the fillets to warm serving plates or a platter, letting the cooking liquid drain back into the pan. Strain the liquid into a clean saucepan and boil briskly until it is reduced to half its volume. Scald the cream; bring it to the boiling point but remove from heat the instant bubbles begin to form where the cream touches the side of the saucepan. Strain the cream into the reduced pan-liquid and stir briskly; remove at once from heat. Divide the sauce over the fillets.

Traditionally, each fillet is garnished with a pair of lightly-sautéed mushroom buttons, put on top of them before saucing. Serves 4.

## Pike Fillets Meunière

4 large pike fillets
1 cup light cream or evaporated milk diluted 2½ parts milk to 1 part water
½ teaspoon salt
⅛ teaspoon freshly-ground white pepper
1 cup flour (approximately)
3 tablespoons butter (no substitutes)
1 teaspoon lemon juice
1 teaspoon chopped fresh parsley
½ teaspoon chopped fresh chervil or ¾ teaspoon dry chervil
Parsley sprigs and lemon wedges for garnish

Wipe or blot the fillets dry. Combine cream, salt and pepper. Dip the fillets in this mixture, then roll in the flour; shake off any excess flour that may cling to them in clots. Sauté the fillets in 2 tablespoons butter over low to moderate heat, cooking about 4 minutes per side, until they are a rich, golden brown. Drain from the pan with a slotted spatula, letting the fat return to the pan, and put on a warmed platter or individual serving plates. Add the remaining butter to the pan and increase the heat. When it froths, dash in the lemon juice, parsley and chervil, stir quickly and briskly, and pour over the fillets. Garnish with parsley sprigs and lemon wedges. Serves 4.

## Baked Pike Fillets

4 large or 8 small pike fillets
4 tablespoons olive oil (or substitute drawn
    butter, page 32)
1 tablespoon lemon juice
Large pinch salt
Small dash freshly-ground white pepper
¼ cup butter or solid margarine
2 tablespoons minced fresh parsley

Marinate the fillets 30 minutes in a marinade
made by mixing the oil, lemon juice, salt, and
pepper. Turn once or twice. If drawn butter is
used in place of olive oil, put the bowl containing the marinade in a warm place so the
butter will not harden. Drain the fillets. Rub
a thin film of butter on the bottom of a heavy
skillet and bring it to high heat. Sear the fillets
not more than 20 to 30 seconds per side, then
arrange them in a well-buttered baking dish.
Melt half the remaining butter, pour over the
fillets, and sprinkle them with parsley. Cook
uncovered in a preheated 350-degree oven for
15 minutes. Baste with the remaining butter
two or three times while the fillets cook.
Serves 4.

## Bourride of Pike

1½ quarts water
¾ teaspoon salt
2 large, sweet onions, peeled and chopped
    coarsely
3 red-ripe tomatoes or the equivalent in
    canned tomatoes, coarsely chopped.

2 **cloves garlic, peeled and minced or mashed**
2 **pounds pike fillets cut into ½-inch strips**
2 **generous dashes orange bitters, or the zest**
 **of ½ orange cut into toothpick-sized strips**
 **(The zest of citrus fruit is the thin outer**
 **peel with all white pith removed.)**
2 **egg yolks**
4 **thick slices toasted French or Italian bread**

Bring the water containing the salt, onion, tomatoes and garlic to a boil and cook briskly for 10 minutes. Reduce to a simmer, add the strips of pike and the bitters or orange zest, and cook 5 to 7 minutes, until the fish flakes readily. Drain the liquid from the pot into a clean saucepan, put the solids in a warmed bowl, and remove the strips of orange zest, if this has been used. Beat the egg yolks into the liquid in the saucepan over very low heat. With a pastry blender or wire potato masher, quickly reduce the solids to a smooth paste and blend them with the liquid in the saucepan, stirring briskly. Put slices of bread into soup bowls and pour the bourride over them. Serves 4.

## Broiled Dilled Pickerel

4-**pound pickerel, or two fish of about 2**
 **pounds each**
2 **tablespoons butter or solid margarine**
2 **tablespoons lemon juice**
½ **teaspoon salt**
⅛ **teaspoon cayenne**
1 **tablespoon dillseed**
1 **large dill pickle**

Cut slits at an angle across the pickerel's body an inch or so apart, on both sides of the fish. Combine the butter and lemon juice, work this into the cuts generously, and rub the entire body of the fish with it, inside and out. Dust the fish, including cavity, with salt and cayenne. Put a big pinch of dillseed and the dill pickle into the cavity; close it with skewers or by sewing. Work the remaining dillseed into the butter mixture packed into the slits, spreading them open to fill generously. Preheat the broiler 5 minutes. Broil the pickerel 7 to 10 minutes per side, depending upon its size; use the tests on page 23 to determine when cooking is completed. Serve with a garnish of lemon wedges. (If you cook two small fish instead of one large one, the adjustment of recipe quantities is easy to make; so is the adjustment of cooking time.) Serves 4.

## Royal Pickerel Fillets

3 cups *court-bouillon* (page 47)
1 tablespoon butter
4 large pickerel fillets or 8 small fillets
16 small mushroom buttons
3 cups raw potato balls
¾ to 1 cup Sauce Velouté (page 168)
2 tablespoons good cognac
Large pinch cayenne

Boil the *court-bouillon* briskly until it is reduced in volume by one-third, reduce heat, and when it simmers, stir in the butter. Poach the fillets in this liquid for 5 to 7 minutes, depending upon their thickness. Parboil the mushroom buttons and potato balls in lightly salted water for 3 minutes, drain well, and transfer to a scantily-buttered skillet over low heat; cook until the mushrooms are tender and the potato balls crusty brown. Drain the fillets and put them on warmed individual service plates; put the mushroom buttons on top of the fillets and arrange the potato balls around the fillets. Warm the Sauce Velouté, stir the brandy and cayenne into it, pour over the fillets, and glaze under the broiler for a moment or two. Serves 4.

## Pickerel Fillets, Seville Style

4 large pickerel fillets
Stingy sprinkling of salt
Generous dusting of cayenne
1 cup orange juice (fresh juice, preferably)
4 tablespoons salt
8 slices of sweet onion, about ½-inch thick
8 slices of firm-ripe (but not soft) tomato
½ green (Bell) pepper, cleaned, cut in matchstick-sized strips
1 tablespoon butter (no substitutes)
Large dash orange bitters

Thirty minutes before cooking time, sprinkle the fillets with salt and cayenne and marinate at room temperature in the orange juice. They should be turned once or twice during the marinating period. At the same time, on a flat surface spread 2 tablespoons salt on waxed paper and press the onion slices into it; sprinkle the remaining 2 tablespoons salt over them. At cooking time, butter a shallow baking dish.

Wash the onion slices under cold running water to remove all salt, and blot them dry. Put the onion slices in the bottom of the pan. Drain the fillets from the orange juice, reserving the juice, and put them on top of the onion slices. Cover the fillets with the tomato slices and strew the slivers of green pepper over the tomatoes. Heat the orange juice, melt the butter in it, add the bitters to the juice, and pour over the fillets. Cook uncovered in a preheated 375-degree oven for 25 minutes, basting occasionally with the pan liquid. Serve with plain boiled rice as a side dish. Serves 4.

## Camp-Style Muskellunge Fillets

2 very large or 4 small muskellunge fillets
8 thick slices of salt pork or fat bacon
2 small sweet onions, peeled and sliced ¼ inch
Dash of pepper
Sprinkling of salt (omit if salt pork is used)
2 tablespoons water
2 tablespoons lemon juice

Trim rinds from the salt pork, blanch by plunging it into boiling water for 3 or 4 minutes, and drain well. Sauté the pork in a heavy skillet until brown on one side. Turn the meat, cover it with the onion slices, and lay the fillets on top of the onions. Sprinkle with pepper. Combine water and lemon juice and pour over the fillets. Cover the pan tightly and cook over moderate heat—20 minutes for large thick fillets, 12 to 15 for small ones. Serves 4.

# Baked Muskellunge Stuffed with Crawfish

6-pound muskellunge or center-cut piece
from a bigger fish
4 cups parboiled crawfish meat
2 eggs, lightly beaten
½ cup chopped mushrooms
½ cup heavy cream or evaporated milk, diluted 3 parts milk to 1 part water
⅓ cup medium-dry Sherry (see page 178)
1½ teaspoon salt
¼ teaspoon freshly-ground white pepper
1½ to 2 cups coarse, fresh breadcrumbs
Butter or solid margarine
¼ cup light cream or evaporated milk, diluted 2½ parts milk to 1 part water
2 tablespoons medium-dry Sherry

If you are cooking a whole fish and have a
pan large enough to handle it, leave the head
on. Grind the crawfish meat, using the coarsest
blade of the grinder, or chop it coarsely. Combine crawfish, eggs, mushrooms, cream, Sherry,
salt and pepper and work this into the breadcrumbs to form a fluffy, light-textured stuffing.
The mixture should be dry rather than soggy.
Stuff the fish, and close the cavity with small
skewers or by sewing. (If cooking a section
from a big fish, close the ends with foil pressed
around the openings and hold with a turn or
two of string.) Butter a baking pan and butter
the outside of the fish. Put fish in pan, and
dust very lightly with salt and pepper. Combine
the cream and Sherry and pour over the fish.

Cook uncovered in a preheated 375-degree oven 45 minutes to 1 hour, depending upon the cross-section thickness; use the tests on page 37 to determine when cooking is completed. Baste with pan juices several times while cooking. Serves 6 to 8.

## Braised Muskellunge Fillets

4 large muskellunge fillets
Head, bones, and trimmings of flesh left after filleting the fish
1 quart cold water
3 cups white Rhine-type wine (see page 178)
2 or 3 sprigs parsley
½ teaspoon shredded fresh thyme or ¾ teaspoon crumbled dry or powdered thyme
2 tablespoons grated sweet onion
½ bay leaf
¼ teaspoon lemon juice or 1 thick slice lemon
2 tablespoons butter (no substitutes)
½ teaspoon salt
Dash of cayenne or small dash Nepal pepper

Put fish head, bones and trimmings in a saucepan with 1 quart cold water, bring to a boil, and boil for 5 minutes; skim off the froth rising to the surface until no more appears. Reduce heat to simmer, and add wine, parsley, onion, bay leaf, and lemon juice or slice. Simmer for 20 minutes from the time simmering re-starts after ingredients are added, and then strain liquid into a clean saucepan through a

fine-meshed cloth. Boil until reduced to half
its volume. Butter a shallow baking dish having a tight-fitting cover. Lay the fillets in this,
and sprinkle with salt and pepper. Add the
remaining butter to the reduced liquid in the
saucepan, and pour over the fillets. Close the
pan; cook in a preheated 350-degree oven for
25 minutes. Serves 4 very satisfactorily.

## Baked Muskellunge Fillets

4 large muskellunge fillets about ½-inch
   thick
2 teaspoons salt
½ teaspoon freshly-ground white pepper
¼ teaspoon powdered thyme
¼ pound butter or solid margarine
2 tablespoons minced, fresh parsley
2 tablespoons minced shallots
⅓ cup lemon juice
¾ cup white, Rhine-type wine (see page 178)

Dry the fillets well; combine the salt, pepper
and thyme and rub them well with this mixture. Butter a shallow casserole, put in the
fillets, and sprinkle the parsley and shallots over
them. Combine lemon juice and wine, and
pour over the fillets. Cover the pan and bake
in a preheated 325-degree oven for 10 minutes.
Open the pan, spread each fillet very thickly
with butter, and cook uncovered for 15 minutes
longer. Serves 4.

## Muskellunge Turbans

2 large muskellunge fillets, 8 inches long and
½ inch thick, cut into 8 strips the length
of the fillets and about 1½ inches wide
4 tablespoons butter or solid margarine
¾ cup chopped, fresh mushrooms
1 tablespoon grated sweet onion
4 tablespoons flour
¼ teaspoon salt
⅛ teaspoon cayenne or half that much Nepal
pepper
½ cup light cream or evaporated milk, diluted 2½ parts milk to 1 part water
8 small mushroom caps, parboiled 3 minutes,
drained
¾ to 1 cup fine, dry breadcrumbs

Butter 8 custard cups or ramekins and coil
the fillets in them; start from the outside and
curl toward the center. Sauté the chopped
mushrooms and onion in the remaining butter
for 3 minutes, then sprinkle the flour and seasonings over them and stir until the flour is
cooked, but not browned—about 3 to 4 minutes.
Add cream and simmer (but do not boil) for
5 to 7 minutes. Divide this sauce over the
fillets in the cups, pouring it into the crevices.
Bake in a preheated 375-degree oven for 35
minutes. Invert the custard cups on ovenproof
serving plates, and lift off the cups. Top each
fillet with a mushroom cap, dust with breadcrumbs, and broil for 2 or 3 minutes, long
enough to brown the breadcrumbs.

Serves 4 hungry people, or 8 who will have something in addition to the fillets to round off their meal.

When looking for other methods of cooking pike, pickerel and muskie, be sure to look over your shoulder. On page 51 there is a recipe for poaching fish in cider which is a wonderful treat if the fish is a sweet-fleshed muskie and, on page 65, a recipe for baking poached fish that works well with any of the *Esox* clan. Looking ahead, try a pike or muskie in the Matelotes on pages 156 and 157, or bake one in the manner recommended for lake trout on page 115. There are others, too, that will please you when adapted, so strike out on your own, experiment and enjoy!

# 8

## TROUT

In the year 63 A. D., the Roman naturalist Pliny the Elder wrote of a tribe of Iberians he observed catching a fish "of very sweet flesh, very shy in its habits," by using a cluster of red feathers tied to their hooks. His description of the fish and the manner in which it was taken leaves little doubt that the Spanish anglers were fishing for trout with flies. For at least 2,000 years, the challenge of the trout has been drawing fishermen, just as it does today.

Yearly, the challenge grows greater as superhighways pierce once-remote areas, and bring about construction of new connecting roads that give access to waters which once could be reached only with considerable effort. At the same time, the increasing pollution of streams that formerly ran clear and cool has narrowed the habitat of all members of the *Salmonidae* family. The trout is very demanding in its requirements, and is either wiser or less adaptable than man. Trout desert a polluted environment; they will not—and cannot—live in warm or dirty water, so the fisherman who wants trout must roam further and climb higher to reach the streams and lakes where the brown, the brook and the rainbow can be found and caught.

Since trout require so much effort to catch, they are certainly worth an equal effort to prepare. And, when the chips are down, it really takes very little more effort to cook trout in a fashion suiting their aristocratic rarity and flavor than it does to roll them in cornmeal and casually toss them into a pan of hot grease.

Take the extra effort, then. You will be repaid by discovering flavors of a delicate subtlety that you may not yet have found in this aristocrat of fishes.

## Trout Bercy

**4 trout of about ¾ pound each**
**½ teaspoon salt**
**Dash of freshly-ground white pepper**
**3 tablespoons butter or solid margarine**
**2 tablespoons chopped shallots**
**1 cup fish stock (page 46)**
**1 cup dry white Burgundy-type wine (see page 178)**

After cleaning, remove heads and fins from fish, trim tails, and sprinkle very lightly with salt and pepper. Melt 1 tablespoon butter in a shallow ovenproof dish, spread the shallots on its bottom, and put the trout on the shallots. Reduce the fish stock to half its volume by boiling briskly, let it cool, and add the wine. Dot the trout with the remaining butter in pea-sized bits, and pour the wine-stock mixture over the fish. Cook uncovered in a preheated 325-degree oven for 12 to 15 minutes. Serves 4.

## Trout à la Bonne Femme

Cook as for Trout Bercy, substituting small button mushrooms for the shallots. Use 1 cup mushrooms, since their flavor is so much less assertive; otherwise, ingredients and procedures are the same.

## Trout Lorraine

4 trout of about ¾ pound each
1 teaspoon salt
Large dash of freshly-ground white pepper
1 teaspoon butter or solid margarine
4 thin slices uncooked ham or 8 slices Canadian bacon
4 tablespoons heavy cream or undiluted evaporated milk
2 teaspoons chopped fresh chives

After cleaning and trimming off heads, tails and fins, dust the fish inside and out with salt and pepper. Butter a shallow baking dish and lay the fish in it. Put a slice of ham or two slices of Canadian bacon on top of each trout. Cook covered in a preheated 350-degree oven for 10 minutes, then pour the cream over the fish and return to the oven uncovered for an additional 8 to 10 minutes. Sprinkle with the chopped chives just before taking the trout to the table. Serves 4.

## Trout Belle Meunière

4 trout of about ¾ pound each
2 to 3 tablespoons flour
½ teaspoon salt
Stingy dash of freshly-ground white pepper
¾ cup milk or evaporated milk diluted with
   equal parts water
1 to 1½ tablespoons olive oil (If you do not
   enjoy the flavor of olive oil, substitute peanut oil or drawn butter, page 32)
1 tablespoon lemon juice
1 tablespoon chopped fresh parsley
1 tablespoon chopped fresh chives
4 tablespoons butter or solid margarine

After cleaning the trout, trim tails and fins.
Combine the flour, salt, and pepper by shaking
them together in a small plastic bag. Wipe
the fish well, dip them in milk, then roll them
in the seasoned flour; shake off any clots of
flour that might cling to them. Heat oil in the
skillet, just the thinnest film of oil covering
the pan's bottom, and sauté the trout over
moderate heat, cooking 4 to 5 minutes per side.
Remove to a warmed platter or individual
serving plates and sprinkle them with lemon
juice, parsley and chives. Pour any excess oil
from the skillet, but do not wipe it dry. Put
in the butter and over high heat brown it
quickly to a warm, dark tan. Divide the butter
over the fish. Garnish with thin lemon slices.
Serves 4.

## Trout Grenoble

Cook as for Trout Meunière, substituting 2 tablespoons well-drained, chopped capers for the parsley-chive garnish, and sautéing ⅓ to ½ cup fine, fresh breadcrumbs in the butter used at the final stage of preparing the dish. Put in the breadcrumbs just as the butter begins to turn color so they do not get too dark.

## Trout in Cream

4 trout of about ¾ pound each
1 teaspoon salt
⅛ teaspoon freshly-ground white pepper
3 tablespoons butter or solid margarine
¼ cup brandy, cognac preferred
1 cup heavy cream or evaporated milk, diluted 2 parts milk to 1 part water

After cleaning the trout, trim tails and fins and dust them lightly inside and out with salt and pepper. Over gentle heat, sauté the fish in the butter, cooking 3 to 4 minutes per side. Heat the brandy, ignite it, and pour it immediately over the fish in the pan. When the flames die down, pour the cream over the fish and cook without boiling for 5 minutes. Divide the pan juices over the fish on warmed serving plates or a platter. Serves 4.

## Trout Spanish Style

4 trout of about ¾ pound each

4 to 6 tablespoons fine, light olive oil (And if you don't like olive oil, please pass up this recipe, as no substitute can give this dish the flavor it requires.)

2 tablespoons flour

½ clove garlic, minced or mashed

¾ cup warm fish stock (page 46)

¾ cup dry white Bordeaux-type wine (see page 178)

*Bouquet garni* tied together with a thread:
   1 bay leaf
   3 or 4 sprigs parsley
   1 sprig fresh thyme

After cleaning the trout, trim off the tails and fins. Heat 1 to 1½ tablespoons of the oil in a skillet—use only enough to cover the pan's bottom with a thin film—and sauté the trout 2 minutes per side, over moderate heat. Transfer the fish to a lightly-oiled, shallow baking dish. Put 4 tablespoons of oil in the skillet, and over low heat stir the flour into it to make a smooth paste. Add the garlic, and let both flour and garlic cook until they are golden tan. Stir occasionally to keep from scorching. Combine the fish stock and wine and pour into the pan while stirring to keep lumps from forming. Put in the *bouquet garni* and allow the mixture to bubble 20 minutes without actually boiling, and stir just often enough to avoid scorching. Take out the herbs, pour the sauce over the trout, and cook covered in a preheated 350-degree oven for 10 minutes. Serves 4.

## Trout Mollau

4 trout of about ¾ pound each
3 tablespoons butter (no substitutes)
2 cups grated sweet onion
1 cup white Rhine-type wine (see page 178)
2 cups fish stock (page 46)
½ teaspoon salt
3 or 4 peppercorns, cracked or nicked with a
   knife
1 bay leaf
4 whole cloves
½ to ¾ cup medium-coarse fresh, soft breadcrumbs
4 tablespoons butter (no substitutes)

After cleaning the trout, trim off tails and fins. Sauté the onion in 3 tablespoons of butter until they begin to become transparent. Add the wine, fish stock and seasonings, and simmer without boiling for 10 minutes. Slip the trout into the pan, being sure the liquid covers them completely. Add more wine and stock if necessary, and then cover the pan and cook 12 to 15 minutes over moderate heat. In a separate skillet, sauté the breadcrumbs in 2 tablespoons of butter until they are a rich gold. Drain the trout and onions from the pan, letting the poaching liquid flow back into the pan, and put the fish on a warmed platter or individual service plates. Bring the liquid in the pan to a brisk rolling boil and cook until it is reduced to half its volume. Strain this sauce into a bowl and quickly stir in the remaining 2 tablespoons of butter to smooth and refine its texture. Divide the sauce over the fish, and sprinkle generously with breadcrumbs. Serves 4.

# Trout in Burgundy

4 trout of about ¾ pound each
1 teaspoon salt
⅛ teaspoon freshly-ground white pepper
Butter or neutral cooking oil
3 tablespoons grated sweet onion
1 bay leaf
1 sprig fennel
2 cups dry, red Burgundy-type wine (see page 178)
3 egg yolks
2 tablespoons lemon juice

After cleaning the fish, trim off heads, tails, and fins; dust very lightly with salt and pepper, inside and out. Butter or oil a baking dish very lightly and arrange the trout on the bottom. Sprinkle the onion over them, and put in the bay leaf and fennel. Bring the wine to a boil and at once pour into the pan over the trout. Cover and cook in a preheated 325-degree oven for 20 to 25 minutes, depending upon the size of the fish. Drain the trout from the pan, letting the liquid run back, and put the fish on a warmed platter or individual serving dishes. Strain the pan liquid into a saucepan and boil briskly until it is reduced to 1 cup. Remove from heat and beat the egg yolks in one at a time. Sprinkle the fish lightly with lemon juice, pour the sauce over them, and serve it forth. Serves 4 quite appetizingly.

## Trout Custard

10 to 12 very thin fillets about 3 by 6 inches
or very thin slices from a large trout with
the bones removed
½ teaspoon salt
Stingy dash of freshly-ground white pepper
4 whole eggs
1½ cups milk or evaporated milk diluted
with equal parts water
¾ teaspoon salt
⅛ teaspoon cayenne or half that much Nepal
pepper
2 cups dead-ripe fresh tomatoes, peeled,
seeded and mashed to a smooth pulp, or
the equivalent in well-drained canned tomatoes, also mashed. It would seem logical
to suppose that tomato paste could be used
here, but please don't. Tomato pastes are
highly seasoned and upset the balance of
flavors in this dish.
Butter or neutral cooking oil
1½ to 2 tablespoons grated Parmesan cheese

Dust the fillets or slices lightly with salt and
pepper, cover a flat surface with cloth and lay
them aside for 10 to 15 minutes. Beat the eggs;
then beat into them the milk, salt, pepper, and
finally the tomatoes. Brush a deep baking dish
with butter or oil and arrange the fillets in it,
allowing plenty of space between and around
them; it may be necessary to cut the fillets into
strips. Pour the egg mixture over the fillets
and cook uncovered in a preheated 325-degree
oven for 30 minutes. Then dust the top with
Parmesan and cook until the cheese is brown

and the custard firmly set. Serve big spoonsful on crisp thin toast. Serves 4 to 6.

### Lake Trout, Kokanee, Coho, Kamloops

These are big trout that swim in the twilight zone between the salmon and steelhead and the small trout of most streams and small lakes. Their flesh is not as delicate as the brook, brown and rainbow, and lacks the high oil content found in salmon. These big fellows respond best to baking; so, too, do the grandpa browns and rainbows that sometimes fall to the lucky angler's lure.

Technically, both the kokanee and coho are salmon, but in their freshwater version require consideration as trout.

### Mushroom-Stuffed Coho

3- to 4-pound coho (or other large trout)
2 tablespoons lemon juice
½ teaspoon salt
Generous dash of freshly-ground white pepper
1½ tablespoons butter or solid margarine
2 cups coarsely-chopped fresh or well-drained canned mushrooms
½ to 1 cup very coarse, dry breadcrumbs
½ teaspoon powdered rosemary
¼ to ½ cup white Rhine-type wine (see page 178)

After cleaning the fish, remove head, trim tail, and take out the fins. If it is necessary to shorten the fish, cut off a section of the tail.

Butter or oil a piece of paper or use a piece of cooking parchment with which to close the opening where the head was removed. Rub the cavity with lemon juice, let stand about 5 minutes, and then dust with salt and pepper. Heat the butter and sauté the mushrooms and breadcrumbs for about 3 minutes. Mix the rosemary with the mushroom-breadcrumb mixture and moisten it with wine; it should be dry and fluffy rather than moist or soggy. Stuff the cavity, close the slit with small skewers or by sewing, and close the head-end with the oiled paper tied with string. Cook uncovered in a lightly-buttered pan in a pre-heated 350-degree oven for 35 to 45 minutes, depending upon thickness. Use the tests given on page 32 to determine when cooking is completed. Serves 4 to 6.

## Kamloops with Tomato Sauce

4 to 5-pound trout
1 teaspoon salt
⅛ teaspoon freshly-ground white pepper
2 tablespoons butter or solid margarine
1 teaspoon flour (approximately)
4 slices bacon
2 cups grated sweet onion
1 clove garlic, minced or mashed
4 cups chopped fresh tomatoes or well-drained canned tomatoes
1 tablespoon chopped fresh parsley
1 teaspoon powdered marjoram or ¾ teaspoon oregano
2 bay leaves
1 cup fish stock (page 46)

After cleaning the fish, if it is necessary, remove head and as much of the tail-end as needed. Wipe fish with a damp cloth, and dust inside and out with salt and pepper. Butter the baking dish, put the fish in it, spread the remaining butter thickly over its top, and sprinkle with flour. Cook uncovered in a pre-heated 375-degree oven for 15 minutes. While the fish cooks, prepare the sauce. Sauté the bacon until it is very crisp, drain, and break into small pieces. In the bacon fat, sauté the onion and garlic until the onion begins to become transparent. Add the tomatoes, seasonings and fish stock; tie the bay leaves with a long string so they can easily be found and removed later. Simmer the sauce 5 minutes, remove bay leaves, pour over the fish in its pan, reduce oven heat to 325 degrees and cook 25 minutes. Baste with the sauce occasionally. Serves 4 to 6.

## Trout Toast

2 cups leftover trout, flaked
½ cup blanched chopped almonds
¼ cup medium-dry Sherry (see page 178)
1 egg yolk
3 tablespoons butter or solid margarine
3 tablespoons flour
1 cup fish stock (page 46)
¼ cup heavy cream or evaporated milk
1 teaspoon salt
¼ teaspoon freshly-ground white pepper
2 egg yolks
4 thick slices crisp toast
Paprika

Soak the flaked fish and almonds in the Sherry for 1 hour, strain, beat the Sherry and one egg yolk together, pour over the fish and almonds, and soak 1 hour longer. Stir occasionally. Melt butter in saucepan; sprinkle the flour over it, and cook over low heat 3 to 4 minutes, stirring to form a smooth paste. Do not let the flour brown. Pour in fish stock and cream, stirring to keep lumps from forming. Add salt and pepper, and then beat in the 2 egg yolks to make a smooth, thick sauce. Add the fish and almonds and the marinade. Let bubble without boiling for 5 minutes, then divide over the toast slices and dust lightly with paprika. Serves 4 as a main course, 6 if there's more to the meal.

## Grayling

The grayling is included here not because it belongs to the trout family, but because it is certainly a spiritual brother to the trout. Today, you must travel far to find grayling, but the trip is worthwhile. Its drama as quarry is matched only by its dramatic impact on the palate. Cook the grayling as you would trout—and vice versa, of course—using the lightest possible touch with the seasonings.

## Grayling in Champagne Sauce

2 grayling of about 1½ pounds each
½ teaspoon salt
A mere suggestion of freshly-ground white pepper

2 cups sliced mushrooms, fresh or canned
½ cup fine, dry breadcrumbs
2 tablespoons butter (no substitute)
2 cups (1 pint) dry Champagne (see page 178)
⅓ cup Sauce Velouté (page 168)

Let the size of your pan and your own taste determine whether or not you trim the fins; the dish will not suffer if they are left on. Rub the fish inside and out with salt and pepper. Chop 1 cup of the mushrooms, heat 1 tablespoon butter, and toss the mushrooms in it for 2 or 3 minutes; add the breadcrumbs, and stir until the crumbs are golden. Stuff the fish with this mixture, closing the cavities with small skewers or by sewing. Heat the remaining butter in a heavy skillet having a tight cover. Spread the remaining mushrooms on its bottom, lay the fish on the mushrooms, and pour in the Champagne. Cover the pan and cook over low heat for 10 minutes; turn the fish and cook 10 minutes longer. Drain the fish and mushrooms from the pan, letting the liquid flow back into the utensil. Arrange fish and mushrooms on a warmed platter. Strain the pan juice, and combine over low heat with the Sauce Velouté. When the sauce is smooth, pour over the fish and serve. Serves 4.

## Grayling *au Bleu*

Though tagged with the name of the grayling (which responds spectacularly to this style of cooking) you can cook any fish—even roughfish

—*au bleu* by using this recipe. There is only one secret to this style of cooking fish, and that is fast work in cleaning them. The fish must be almost alive when it goes into the pot, or the dish will fail. Actually, *au bleu* cooking is a very simple process if you work fast and follow directions explicitly.

> 1 live fish of about 1 pound; the fish *must be alive* when you start to prepare the dish
> 1 quart boiling water
> 2½ tablespoons fresh natural lemon juice or 2 tablespoons white vinegar

Before killing the fish, have the water boiling and the lemon juice or vinegar measured and ready. Stun the fish and clean it quickly. Handle it no more than necessary—the outer mucus coating is vital to this method of cooking. *Do not wash or wipe the fish at any time.* The instant the fish is cleaned, pour the lemon juice or vinegar into the boiling water and slip the fish into the water immediately. Boiling will stop. When it starts again, cover the pan tightly and remove it from heat at once. Let it stand 5 to 6 minutes for a 10-inch fish, 3 to 5 for a smaller one. Cooking is completed when the eyes of the fish pop white from its head. Cook only one fish at a time, and prepare a fresh pan of water with fresh lemon juice or vinegar for each fish cooked; the liquid cannot be re-used. One fish is usually considered a serving.

Trout are the exception to the rule of free interchange of types of fish between recipes; not all methods of cooking are suited for trout. Choose only those using no seasonings or ingredients with flavors so pronounced as to overwhelm the trout's delicate taste. But do experiment. For openers, cook small trout by the muskie recipe on page 100, and that for catfish with sherry sauce on page 70. For baking-sized trout, salmon recipes are always good. These suggestions don't complete the list, but why should you be deprived of the pleasure of discovering others for yourself?

# 9

## ANADROMOUS FISH

A number of kinds of fish divide their time between fresh and salt water, but only a handful are important as "eating" fish, such as the salmon and steelhead, the shad, the striped bass and the sturgeon. Some of the salmon and the striped bass have been persuaded to abandon their migratory habits and spend all their time in fresh water, but this does not change their classification; cook them the same way that you would their travelling cousins.

### Salmon and Steelhead

All salmon belong to the *Salmonidae* family, but there are differences between them. Atlantic salmon belong to the *Salmo* branch and are properly called *Salmo salar*; the Western steelhead, *Salmo irideus gairdneri*, is closer kin to *salar* than is the Western salmon. These belong to the *Oncorhynchus* branch of the big *Salmonidae* family; the sub-species include the kokanee and coho, which have been relocated in many places and caught as freshwater fish.

What's any of this got to do with cooking salmon? A fairly substantial bit. The *Salmos*, Atlantic salmon and steelhead, have a very firm-textured flesh containing light, pleasant-flavored oil; they should be cooked by the most straightforward recipes, using light seasonings and mild sauces. On the other hand, the

*Oncorhynchus* group responds more gracefully to robust seasonings and pronounced sauces. So, let your selection of cooking methods be guided by the kind of salmon you are cooking, in order to get the greatest pleasure at the table.

## Broiled or Grilled Salmon Steaks

*In the kitchen oven*

> **2 large salmon steaks at least 1 inch thick**
> **⅓ cup drawn butter (page 32)**
> **Salt, pepper, lemon wedges, to be used after cooking**

Use a broiler rack; preheat broiler with rack and pan. (Unless the rack is hot, the salmon will stick to it.) Rub the steaks on both sides with drawn butter, cook 6 inches from heat source for 20 minutes, basting frequently with the drawn butter. If a rack is used, reflected heat from the broiler pan makes it unnecessary to turn the steaks. Remove to a warmed platter, slip off skin, divide at the center, and take out bones. Season only after cooking. Serves 4.

*Over the outdoor grill*

> **2 large salmon steaks, 1 inch thick, preferably 1½ inches thick**
> **Paprika**
> **½ cup drawn butter (page 32)**
> **Salt, pepper, lemon wedges, to be used after cooking**

Have the coals glowing dully, not a brilliant red or yellow. Wipe the steaks with a damp cloth and rub both surfaces with paprika. This will not affect the flavor of fish cooked over direct heat from coals, but prevents overly rapid cooking and a charred outside layer of flesh. With the grill 6 to 8 inches above the coals, cook 7 to 8 minutes per side. Brush occasionally with drawn butter. Remove to warm platter, slip off skin, and take out bones. Serve with salt, pepper and lemon wedges and let each one season his own portion. Serves 4.

## To broil or grill whole salmon

On a rack in a broiler pan, cook 6 to 8 inches from the heat source; allow 12 to 14 minutes per inch of thickness. Reflected heat makes turning unnecessary.

On the outdoor grill over coals, rub the skin with butter, then with paprika; this is not necessary when cooking in the oven, as neither gas nor electric heat is as drying as live coals. Have the grill 10 inches above dull coals, and cook 15 minutes per side.

Indoors or out, use the tests on page 37 to determine when the fish is completely cooked.

## Salmon Steaks Nantaise

2 salmon steaks about 1½ inches thick
3 thin slices sweet onion
1 small carrot, peeled and sliced paper-thin
1 clove garlic, minced or mashed
½ teaspoon salt

4 or 5 cracked peppercorns (or nick them
  with a knife)
2 whole cloves
2 bay leaves
3 or 4 sprigs fresh parsley
2 or 3 celery sprigs with leaves
3 to 4 cups milk or evaporated milk diluted
  with equal parts water
4 egg yolks
1 egg
2 tablespoons lemon juice
¾ cup blanched, shredded almonds

Wrap the steaks in cheesecloth so they can
be lifted from the pan without breaking after
being cooked. Lay the steaks in a deep, lightly-
oiled skillet, add the onion, carrot, all seasonings and herbs, and pour in the milk. The
steaks should be completely covered with milk.
Bring to a boil; reduce to a simmer, and cook
25 minutes from the time simmering starts.
Lift out the steaks, remove skin and bones,
and put on warmed individual serving plates.
Strain 1½ cups of the poaching liquid into a
saucepan over very low heat, or into the top
of a double boiler over boiling water. Beat
the egg yolks and eggs, and pour slowly and
steadily into the hot milk while beating with
a wire whisk or slotted spoon. Cook for 5
minutes after the addition of the eggs; do not
allow to boil. Remove from heat, add the almonds and lemon juice, blend well, and divide
the sauce over the fish. The traditional garnish

for this dish is a dab of hard-cooked egg yolk crumbled over each serving. Serves 4.

### Dilled Pickled Salmon (*Gravad Lox*)

8-pound center cut of a large salmon, in one
  piece
1 tablespoon peppercorns, white or black
1 tablespoon allspice berries
1 cup Kosher Sour Salt (if not available, use
  fine ice-cream salt; the grains should be
  about the size of No. 4 shot-pellets)
⅓ cup sugar
½ cup cognac, akavit, or vodka
Large bunches of fresh or dried dill

Leave the skin on the salmon, but cut along the backbone and remove backbone and ribs (see page 11). Wipe the pieces of fish with a damp cloth. Crush the peppercorns and allspice berries into coarse pieces; they should not be ground or powdered. Combine all the seasonings and coat all surfaces of the fish, pressing them into skin and flesh so they will adhere. Sprinkle all surfaces with the liquor. Place the fish in a deep china or glass bowl, or an enameled pan without breaks or chipped spots in it. Wash the dill and shake it dry, but leave some moisture clinging to it. Put one-third of the dill in the pan, and lay a piece of the salmon on it, skin down. Spread a thick layer of dill on the salmon, and put the other piece on it, flesh down. Use the remaining third of the dill to cover the salmon. Place a heavy plate or clean board on top of the salmon and weight it to press down the fish. Refrigerate for 36 hours—48 hours is better. Turn the salmon two or three times during this period; a liquid will form in the bowl, and some of it should be spooned between the two layers when the fish is turned. Wipe the fish with a damp cloth before serving in thin slices. Salmon prepared in this fashion can be stored up to 10 days in the refrigerator.

## Shad

Though many of the once-great shad rivers no longer yield fish in the thousands and tens of thousands during the shad's spawning run, there are still enough streams and shad to give anglers action, if they catch the runs on time.

If you are lucky, your catch will include a female or two, heavy with roe; and by all means take advantage of the recipes using the roe as a dish in its own right, or in the sauce. Most of the recipes given for black bass can be successfully used with shad, as can some of those for roughfish. At least they offer a change from the customary baked planked shad.

## Baked Planked Shad

*In the kitchen oven*

  1 shad per two servings
  Salt and pepper
  Drawn butter (page 32)

Clean the fish from the back (see page 11). Remove head, tail, and fins. Use an inch-thick plank of oak, ash or hickory, well-greased on the cooking side. Preheat the plank while preheating the oven to 450 degrees. Place the shad on the plank, skin side down, sprinkle with salt and pepper, and brush with drawn butter. Bake at 450 degrees for 15 minutes, basting with the drawn butter once or twice. Reduce heat to 350 degrees and cook 10 to 15 minutes longer, depending upon the thickness of the fish; baste two or three times during this period of cooking. Serve with lemon wedges. Allow 1 fish per two servings.

*Over an outdoor fire*

**1 shad per two servings**
**3 long strips of bacon per shad cooked**
**Salt, pepper, and lemon wedges for seasoning after cooking**

Clean the fish from the back (see page 11). Have a bed of coals at least 6 inches deep, medium-red, with no flames. Use a plank of oak, ash or hickory 1 to 1½ inches thick. Grease the cooking side and preheat the plank by leaning it over the coals for 15 or 20 minutes before using. Lay the shad on the plank, skin side down, and put strips of bacon across the fish at top, middle, and bottom. Nail bacon and fish to the plank with non-galvanized roofing nails. Prop the plank on stones or stakes so it leans over the coals about 20 inches from them. Cook 30 to 35 minutes, and then reverse the plank end-for-end and cook for another 30 minutes; this allows the fish to cook evenly. There are so many variables of wind conditions and air temperatures in outdoor cooking that precise timing is difficult to give. The bacon strips make the fish self-basting and self-seasoning; serve with salt, pepper, and lemon wedges and let each person season his own. Allow 1 fish per two servings.

Other fish can be plank cooked outdoors or in the kitchen range by this method. The methods of cooking and seasoning also apply to fish cooked under the kitchen broiler without the plank, or on an outdoor grill. However, cooking time should be cut by about one-half.

## Broiled Shad Roes

4 roes
1 teaspoon salt
¼ teaspoon pepper
1 teaspoon lemon juice
2 tablespoons melted butter (no substitutes)
1 teaspoon lemon juice
Toast slices

Wipe the roe with a damp cloth, dust with salt and pepper, and sprinkle with lemon juice. Combine the melted butter with the 1 teaspoon lemon juice. Broil the roe 5 minutes per side, basting with the butter-lemon juice mixture.

Split the roe, put them open side up on toast slices, and brush them with the remaining basting liquid. The usual garnish with each serving is a strip or two of crisp bacon and a few lemon wedges. Serves 4.

## Broiled Shad with Roe Sauce

3- to 4-pound shad, broiled or grilled according to recipe on page 130
Roe from shad
2 tablespoons butter or solid margarine
1 tablespoon chopped shallots
1½ tablespoons flour
¾ cup heavy cream or undiluted evaporated milk
2 egg yolks
½ teaspoon salt
Large dash pepper
½ to ¾ cup buttered fresh breadcrumbs

While the fish is cooking, drop the roe into a pan of boiling water for 3 minutes, to firm it. Drain and split the case. Heat the butter in a saucepan, add the shallots, and cook for 5 minutes over gentle heat; stir occasionally to prevent scorching. Put the roe in the pan and sprinkle it with the flour. Slowly add the cream while stirring; cook for 5 minutes without allowing the cream to boil. Remove from heat, and beat in the egg yolks and seasoning. Keep the sauce warm until the shad is placed on a warmed platter, pour the sauce over the fish, sprinkle breadcrumbs thickly over the top, and put under the broiler long enough to crisp and brown the breadcrumbs. Serves 4.

## Loire Fisherman's Shad

4 to 5-pound shad, or a pair of smaller fish
1 quart cold water
1 pint Barsac or Sauterne (these are the wines traditionally used in the recipe; for substitutes see page 178)
2 tablespoons white wine vinegar
1 bay leaf
3 sprigs celery tops with leaves
3 or 4 peppercorns, cracked or nicked with a knife
1 clove garlic, mashed or sliced paper-thin
½ pound butter (no substitutes)
1 tablespoon chopped shallots
½ teaspoon salt
⅛ teaspoon freshly-ground white pepper
1 tablespoon white wine vinegar
1½ tablespoons flour

Remove fins and tail from the cleaned fish, and take off the head if necessary to make it fit the cooking-pan. Put the water, wine, vinegar, bay leaf, celery, peppercorns and garlic in the pan, bring to a quick rolling boil, reduce to a simmer and put in the fish. Cover and cook for 15 minutes, remove from heat, and set aside, leaving the fish to cook in the hot liquid. It should stand for at least 30 minutes, 45 minutes if a big fish. Melt the butter in a saucepan over low heat and sauté the shallots until they begin to soften; sprinkle them with salt and pepper. Strain ¾ cup of the liquid from the cooking pot, and blend the vinegar with it. Sprinkle the flour over the shallots and cook 3 to 4 minutes; do not let the flour brown. Stir the ¾ cup fish broth and vinegar into the shallots and simmer for 2 or 3 minutes. Drain the fish from the pot onto a warm platter and pour the sauce over it. (If the fish being cooked was a female containing roe, cook the roe by the recipe on page 129 to serve with the shad; or, simply flatten the roe and sauté in drawn butter.) Serves 4 to 6.

## Baked Stuffed Shad, Plantation Style

4-pound shad
Bacon dripping, or a neutral cooking oil
3 slices bacon, diced
¾ cup diced celery
3 tablespoons chopped sweet onion
3 tablespoons butter or solid margarine
3 cups hard, dry bread cut in small dice
2 or 3 sprigs fennel
1½ teaspoons salt
½ teaspoon pepper
½ cup fish stock (page 46)

Trim off fins and tail and wipe the shad dry; rub well, inside and out, with bacon dripping or oil. Sauté the bacon with the onion and celery until the vegetables are done, but still soft. Add the butter and bread, and cook until the bread begins to tan, stirring so the pieces cook evenly. Stir in the fennel, salt, and pepper, and moisten with the fish stock. Stuff the shad, and close the cavity with small skewers or by sewing. Bake on a rack in a shallow pan in a preheated 325-degree oven for 45 minutes. Serves 4 to 6.

## Striped Bass

To each angler, the striped bass is a fish of different aspects: Atlantic seaboarders think of it as a surf fish; Pacific coast dwellers see it as a fish of the brackish tidal rips of the river mouths and bays. For years, these were the only two areas where stripers abounded. Now, though, the striped bass has moved inland, to the huge freshwater lakes created by man. Santee-Cooper in South Carolina and Texoma, on the Texas-Oklahoma border, are only two of the many spots that cause fishermen's eyes to light up when stripers are mentioned.

Freshwater or brackish, the striped bass retains the classification of an anadromous fish. Those from landlocked lakes have less fat in their somewhat grainy flesh than do their seagoing brothers, but all stripers are rather oily when cooked. This indicates the use of a grill rack when oven-baking or broiling, and for sturdy seasonings when cooking the striper in a stew or chowder. It also calls for discarding any liquid in which a striped bass has been poached, rather than using it as base for a sauce, and for avoiding the skillet or sauté-pan when preparing the fish. With these precautions observed, the striper can be cooked by many other recipes than the few which follow.

## Grilled Striped Bass Steaks

4 striped bass steaks, ¾ to 1 inch thick
¾ teaspoon salt
Dash of Nepal pepper (cayenne can be substituted)
6 or 8 thick slices from medium-sized sweet
onion
3 or 4 sprigs fresh parsley
1 large sprig fresh thyme or ½ teaspoon
powdered thyme
2 whole cloves
½ bay leaf
1½ cups dry white Bordeaux-type wine (see
page 178)
1 teaspoon lemon juice
2 cups cold water
1 cup Sauce Aurore (page 167)

Wipe the steaks dry, and dust with salt and
pepper. Put the onion, parsley, thyme, cloves,
and bay leaf in the bottom of a heavy skillet
and combine the wine, lemon juice and water,
pouring it over them. The liquid should come
to almost the top of the steaks, but not quite
cover them. Cover the pan, and cook 15 to 20
minutes over medium heat, until the flesh of
the bass parts easily from the backbone. Drain
steaks from the pan, remove skin and backbone, and put on a platter or individual
warmed serving plates. Pour the Sauce Aurore
over the fish, and glaze for 1 or 2 minutes
under the broiler. Serves 4.

# Striped Bass Steaks Genovese

2 large steaks 1½ inches thick from a large bass, or 4 steaks of that thickness taken from a smaller fish
½ cup olive oil (If you don't care for olive oil, cook the fish another way; no other oil can be used to give this dish its traditional character.)
4 cloves garlic
½ cup fresh basil or ¾ cup dry basil
½ cup fresh parsley leaves, coarse stems discarded
½ teaspoon salt
4 walnut halves
6 mint leaves

Brush the steaks lightly with olive oil and broil them on a rack, about 6 inches from the heat source, for 12 to 15 minutes. (If cooked on the outdoor grill over coals, the timing is 6 minutes per side.) Baste occasionally with fresh oil as the fish cooks—never use the pan drippings to baste with. Prepare the sauce by pounding together in a mortar ⅓ cup of the oil, the garlic, basil, parsley, salt, walnuts, and mint. Work it into a smooth, creamy paste. If you have a blender, the sauce is easy; just put it in the blender and run at high speed in 10 to 15-second bursts until the desired smoothness is achieved. Three or four minutes before cooking is completed, remove the steaks, brush both sides thickly with the sauce, and return to the broiler to finish. Serves 4 who are willing to ignore the frowns of friends for 48 hours.

## Sturgeon

Now, we move into the realm of giants. Even a small sturgeon is big, and large sturgeon are very big indeed. Today's biggest sturgeon are taken from such famous streams as Idaho's Snake River, California's Klamath and Sacramento, Canada's St. Lawrence, and the midwest's Ohio; and it's very likely that the biggest fish in a good sturgeon river are never caught, simply because they are so big. The record sturgeon tilted the scales at something over 1100 pounds, and there are stories of sturgeon of yesterday so big that a horse team was needed to haul them up on the bank.

For all its size, this armored survivor from prehistory has delicious, though somewhat oily, flesh. Italian commercial fishermen working their salmon nets in the waters of Suisun Bay in the days before 1954, when California lifted its ban on taking sturgeon, used to smuggle ashore and share with friends the occasional small sturgeon that got entangled. Their good advice to novices at sturgeon cooking I now pass on to you: never cook a piece of sturgeon in a skillet, or in a baking pan without a rack to hold the flesh away from the oil that will drip during cooking. Observe this precaution when selecting recipes other than those that follow for the preparation of sturgeon.

## Sturgeon Steaks Mirabeau

4 sturgeon steaks about 6 inches square by
    1 inch thick
1 teaspoon salt

¾ teaspoon coarsely-ground black pepper
⅓ teaspoon paprika
8 anchovy fillets, partly drained
8 or 10 stuffed green olives


Mix the salt, pepper and paprika, and rub into the steaks on both sides. Broil on a rack 6 inches from the heat source. Cook for 10 to 12 minutes; reflected heat from the pan below the rack makes it unnecessary to turn the steaks. Remove to a heatproof platter or service plates which have been warmed. Split the anchovy fillets lengthwise, arrange them in criss-cross pattern on each steak, dot the diamonds formed by the fillets with olives, and return to the broiler for 2 or 3 minutes. Serves 4.


## Baked Stuffed Sturgeon

4- to 5-pound piece of sturgeon cut so it will be 3 to 4 inches thick
1 teaspoon salt
¼ teaspoon coarsely-ground black pepper
½ cup white wine vinegar
1 cup fish stock (page 46)
3 or 4 tarragon leaves, fresh or dry; dry leaves should be steeped for a few minutes in a cup of water containing ¼ teaspoon vinegar
4 thick slices from a large, sweet onion
3 large firm cucumbers peeled deeply and sliced lengthwise
1 cup Sauce Bercy (page 175)

Prepare the stuffing in advance by mixing the vinegar and fish stock, stirring into it the salt and pepper, and soaking in this liquid the tarragon leaves, onion and cucumber. Marinate for at least an hour, with an occasional stirring. When removing the onion and cucumber, drain as much of the marinade as possible back into the bowl. Cut a pocket in the side of the piece of sturgeon and slide into this opening the onion and cucumber slices. Rub the outside of the roast generously with the marinade liquid. Cook uncovered, on a rack in a baking pan, in a preheated 350-degree oven for 45 minutes to 1 hour, until the flesh flakes easily. Baste with the marinade liquid several times while the roast cooks—do not use the pan juices for basting. Have the Sauce Bercy warm when cooking is completed. Transfer the roast to a warmed platter, slice, and then cover with the sauce. Serves 6 to 8.

Elsewhere in the book, you will find other recipes suitable for use in preparing the anadromous fish. In making your selection, recall the notes of caution that go with the paragraphs introducing you to each of these fish. There are many recipes that can be successfully adapted with minor changes in cooking times and procedures, such as using a rack when broiling or baking, discarding marinades and poaching liquids, and making fresh sauce with which to dress your fish. So, to substitute, proceed with caution—but do proceed.

# 10

## ROUGH FISH

No effort's going to be made here to settle the endless discussion between fishermen about which species should be classed as "rough fish." By observation, the classification seems to vary from one part of the country to another. Where trout are plentiful, black bass are sometimes frowned upon as rough fish; where bass rule, the carp gets kicked into the rough fish cellar, and so it goes. And in areas where good fishing of any kind is rare, almost every fish available from local waters is considered a sports or game fish.

Generally speaking, the rough fish rating is given to those varieties that are most difficult to cook. If you are willing to take the trouble, you will find that nearly every freshwater fish has some redeeming feature that can be brought out by proper handling in the kitchen. Finding that redeeming feature can be a challenge for the dedicated fisherman who is disadvantaged by having to live where only rough fish swim. It can also be one of the most rewarding aspects of fish cookery.

Because rough fish present pretty much the same culinary problems, recipes suitable for one species are almost always suitable for others.

## Carp

Because the carp thrives in warmer water than will support such species as trout and bass, and is primarily a bottom-feeding vegetarian, it is relatively easy to hook and presents only a sluggish resistance. Thus, the carp gets a low rating from anglers as a sport fish. Because it lives in warm water, its flesh is soft. Since it is also bony, the carp gets a low rating as an eating fish. Outside of using the lightest tackle when fishing for them, there's little the angler can do to improve the carp's reputation as a game fish. The chef, though, can do a lot.

One way to improve the carp's flavor is to keep the fish alive for several days in a big tub or barrel of fresh water, after they are caught. A hose running slowly into the container will provide the fresh oxygen they need. During this time, feed the carp a neutral diet, such as bread or cornmeal. This purges any muddy or foreign flavors from their flesh.

While the second method sounds cruel, it is very practical and extremely simple. It simply consists of bleeding the carp to death rather than tapping them with a priest. Hang the carp by the lips, and cut out their vents in a deep V-cut. Let them hang until they no longer bleed, clean and scale them, and after scaling scrape their bodies with the back of a knife blade to remove all mucus. Cut out the skin around the fins, too, for this is where the warm water algae cling and defy scraping or scrubbing.

Combine the two procedures, and carp will taste like a different fish.

## Carp in Red Wine

3- to 4-pound carp, cleaned and scaled
1 teaspoon salt, ½ teaspoon pepper
6 slices bacon, cut very thick
2 tablespoons butter (no substitutes)
2 tablespoons flour
1 tablespoon minced celery root (celeriac)
3 sprigs fresh parsley, 2 whole cloves
6 peppercorns, cracked or nicked with a knife
1 bay leaf, 4 thin slices lemon
3 cups fish stock (page 46)
2 cups dry red Bordeaux-type wine (see page 178)
1 tablespoon butter (no substitutes)

Dust the fish inside and out with salt and pepper, and let it rest for 10 to 15 minutes. Dice the bacon and sauté slowly in a heavy pan, big and deep enough to hold the fish. Knead flour and butter into a smooth paste and flake into the cooking bacon, stirring occasionally to keep the flour from turning brown. Put in all remaining ingredients except the wine and 1 tablespoon butter in the pan and let the liquid boil; reduce to a simmer and slip the carp in. Cook for 15 minutes. Pour in the wine, and when the liquid simmers again, cook 20 minutes. Remove the carp, skin it, and flake off its flesh in large pieces. Strain the liquid from the pot through a cloth into a clean saucepan, put in the pieces of carp, bring to a boil, remove from heat, and stir in the final tablespoon of butter. Serve in a deep bowl. Boiled potatoes are the traditional accompaniment. Serves 4.

## Russian-Style Carp, Cucumber Sauce

4 steaks from a large carp, cut 1½ inches
  thick
½ teaspoon freshly-ground black pepper
1 clove garlic
8 anchovy fillets
2 large firm cucumbers
2 tablespoons salt
¾ cup melted butter or margarine
1 tablespoon brandy—preferably cognac
Large pinch freshly-ground black pepper

Remove skin from the steaks, wipe them with
a damp cloth, and rub with pepper. Drop the
garlic clove into a tablespoon or two of boiling
water to soften it, then mash it with the
anchovies into a smooth paste. (Anchovy paste
can be used; if it is, reduce the quantity of salt
by ½ teaspoon.) Spread both sides of the steaks
with the anchovy mixture, and broil on a rack
6 inches from the heat source for 15 minutes.
It will not be necessary to turn the steaks; reflected heat from the broiler pan will cook the
bottom side. Peel the cucumbers, slice them
very thin, and remove the pulpy centers and
seeds. Press the slices into the salt, shake to remove any excess, and then put the cucumbers in
a bowl; cover them with boiling water and let
stand for 10 minutes. Drain well. Stir the melted
butter and brandy together, add the pepper,
pour over the cucumbers, and mash with a
wooden spoon into a smooth sauce. Remove the
carp steaks from the broiler, put them on
warmed plates, and divide the sauce over them.
Serves 4.

## Japanese-Style Carp

3- to 4-pound carp, cleaned and scaled

2 cups fish stock (page 46)

½ cup soy sauce (take the trouble to get a good imported sauce, such as Kikkoman, instead of the watery, pale, domestic versions, which are about half as potent as they should be)

3 gratings of fresh ginger or ¾ teaspoon powdered ginger

1 teaspoon peanut oil

¼ cup soy sauce

2 tablespoons rice vinegar (or, substitute white wine vinegar)

½ cup Sake (or substitute Sauterne)

Combine the fish stock and ½ cup soy sauce, and add the ginger, (poach the carp in this) with the liquid barely simmering. Cook for 25 to 30 minutes, depending upon the size of the fish. Drain, skin, and remove flesh from the bones of the carp. In a saucepan over very low heat, combine the peanut oil, ¼ cup soy sauce, vinegar and wine. Simmer 5 minutes without letting it boil, add the pieces of fish, cook 5 minutes, serve over boiled rice. Serves 6 to 8.

## Sweet and Sour Carp

4 slices from a large carp, cut about 1½ inches thick
4 egg yolks
5 tablespoons cornstarch
2 tablespoons sweet Sherry (see page 178)
½ teaspoon salt
½ cup flour
Fat for deep frying—preferably peanut oil
4 tablespoons leaf lard or solid shortening
½ cup fish stock (page 46)
6 tablespoons cider vinegar
4 tablespoons sugar
2 tablespoons grated fresh ginger, or 4 tablespoons powdered ginger
1 teaspoon soy sauce (again, use a full-strength import instead of the pale domestic version)
1⅓ tablespoons cornstarch
⅓ cup cold water

Dry the fish slices well, skin them, and score their surfaces lightly. Combine egg yolks, cornstarch, Sherry and salt, beating into a smooth, creamy liquid. Dip the pieces of fish in this, and roll them in flour; shake off any excess that clings. Fry in deep fat for 10 minutes, until nicely browned. Drain on cloth or paper towels. In a saucepan, heat the lard about 2 minutes past its melting stage, over low heat, and then beat in the fish stock, vinegar, sugar, ginger and soy sauce. Let simmer for 5 minutes. Dissolve the cornstarch in cold water and beat briskly into the simmering sauce. Serve the sauce over the fried fish slices. Serves 4 quite surprisingly.

### Blackfish or Bowfin

These are the proper names of the fish known variously, according to the region in which it is caught, as the grindle, grind, grinder, cottonfish, choupiquel, mudfish, speckled cat, or scaled ling. Like the sturgeon, the blackfish is a survivor from prehistoric times; its form has not changed since the days of the dinosaurs.

Blackfish are widely distributed. They are voracious and carnivorous, and often wind up getting hooked on baits intended for other fish. It is quite probable that you will encounter blackfish, if you have not already done so, and with the following recipes or any of those designed to tame rough fish, you are prepared to deal with the fish by whatever name you call it.

## Louisiana-Style Choupiquel

2 to 3-pound fish, cleaned, scaled, head and
  fins removed
1½ to 2 quarts fish stock (page 46)
4 or 5 hot red peppers—the small chili Japonais or Tepine
½ lime, sliced thin
3 tablespoons butter or solid margarine
1 tablespoon minced green onion, including
  tops
½ teaspoon salt
Dash of cayenne or Nepal pepper
⅛ teaspoon paprika
4 tablespoons flour
2 cups hot, freshly-cooked rice

Poach the fish in the stock, to which has been added the hot red peppers and the lime slices. Cook at a simmer for 25 to 30 minutes, depending upon the size of the fish. Remove from stock, drain well, skin, and flake flesh from bones, reserving flesh in a hot covered bowl. Melt butter in a deep skillet and sauté the onion until the green tops are limp and beginning to darken. Add salt, pepper and paprika, then sprinkle the flour over the onion, and stir until it is all combined with the fat. Strain 1½ cups of the poaching liquid and slowly pour it into the skillet, stirring to keep lumps from forming as the liquid combines with the flour. Add the fish to the sauce, stir in the hot cooked rice, let simmer for 3 or 4 minutes, and serve in a deep bowl or individual soup bowls. Serves 6 generously—8 at a pinch.

## Grinder in Tomato Sauce

2½ to 3-pound fish, cleaned, scaled, and skinned
3 raw potatoes peeled and sliced ¼ inch
1½ cups tomato juice
½ cup lime juice
1 cup fish stock (page 46)
1 clove garlic, minced fine
⅓ cup chopped fresh parsley
1½ teaspoons salt
⅛ teaspoon cayenne or ¼ teaspoon Nepal pepper
1 tablespoon butter or solid margarine
¾ to 1 cup medium-fine fresh breadcrumbs

Cut the cleaned, skinned fish into slices about 1 inch thick; cut at right angles to the body. Butter a deep casserole and lay a slice of potatoes on its bottom, then a layer of fish slices; build up the pot this way, leaving plenty of room between pieces of fish and potato, and topping with a layer of potato slices. Combine all remaining ingredients except the butter and breadcrumbs and pour into the casserole. There should be ¼ to ½ inch of liquid over the top layer of potato slices; if not, add more stock and tomato juice. Cook in a preheated 375-degree oven for 45 minutes, with the casserole covered loosely. Do not add additional liquid. Sauté the breadcrumbs in the butter and spread them over the top during the final few minutes of cooking to let them brown crisply. Serves 6 to 8.

## Spiced Blackfish

- 3- to 4-pound blackfish, cleaned, scaled, head and fins removed
- 2 quarts fish stock (page 46)
- 2 cups cider vinegar
- 1½ teaspoons whole cloves
- 1 teaspoon cracked allspice berries
- 10 peppercorns, cracked or nicked with a knife
- ½ teaspoon salt

Put the fish in the cold stock, bring to a boil, skim froth, reduce to a simmer, and cook 25 to

30 minutes, depending upon its size. Drain, skin, and put in a long, shallow dish. Strain 1 cup of the poaching liquid into a clean saucepan, add all remaining ingredients, bring to a boil, reduce to a simmer, and let cook for 5 minutes. Pour over the fish, cover the dish tightly by pressing foil over it and down its sides. Let stand for 2 hours. From time to time, stir the liquid and spoon some over the fish. Remove and drain the fish; serve cold with Mayonnaise (page 172) or Hollandaise (page 171) or one of the bland white sauces given in Chapter 12. Or, combine with a sauce and use as a canape spread. Serves 6 as a main course, more in canape form.

## Drumfish

Also called the freshwater drum, to distinguish it from its bigger seagoing cousins, the drumfish is called by the name of another saltwater fish of anadromous habits, the sheepshead. Its regional names include gasperoo, gaspergou, and just plain gou—also, thunderpumper and crocus. If you have any doubt about the real identity of the drum, it is the fish with the "lucky bone." Its earbones have a natural formation which makes them look as if they had been stamped with the letter "L," which some hopeful anglers interpret as meaning "luck."

Your success in cooking drumfish depends upon the use of a recipe that is suited both to your taste and the fish. If the following few don't appeal to you, look at others which have proved successful with rough fish.

## Baked Devilled Drum

3- to 4-pound fish, cleaned; head, tail and fins removed

2 tablespoons cooking oil, preferably peanut oil

1 teaspoon salt

½ teaspoon cayenne or ¼ teaspoon Nepal pepper

2 tablespoons prepared mustard

1 teaspoon meat extract: **BV, Bovril,** etc.

3 drops Tabasco Sauce

2 tablespoons melted butter or solid margarine

1 tablespoon prepared mustard

Make slashes across the body of the fish, about an inch apart, on both sides of its body. Combine the oil, salt, cayenne, mustard, meat extract and Tabasco, and rub this generously into the cuts, over the body, and inside the cavity; be sure to cover the raw flesh left when the head was cut off. Bake in a well-greased shallow pan, uncovered, in a preheated 350-degree oven for 25 to 30 minutes, depending upon the thickness of the fish. Blend the melted butter and mustard and baste the fish while cooking, alternately basting with the pan juices. Turn the fish at midpoint in the cooking. Serves 6 to 8.

## Gaspergou Chowder, Delta Style

4-pound (approximately) fish, cleaned and
    scaled
1½ quarts cold water
½ teaspoon salt
½ lemon, cut in thin slices
1 tablespoon butter or solid margarine
4 potatoes, peeled and diced ½ inch
3 medium-sized sweet onions sliced ¼ inch
4 cups chopped fresh tomatoes, or canned
    tomatoes; whether fresh or canned, use all
    juices
2 tablespoons dry Vermouth
1 cup medium-dry Sherry (see page 178)
1½ tablespoons lemon juice
2 tablespoons butter or solid margarine

Put the fish in a deep pan, cover with cold
water, bring to a boil, skim froth, and reduce
water to simmer. Add salt and lemon slices,
and cook for 15 to 20 minutes. The fish does not
need to be completely cooked, but done just
enough to make it easy to separate the skin and
flake the flesh off the bones in good-sized pieces.
Reserve the flesh in a deep warmed bowl.
Spread 1 tablespoon butter on the inside of a
deep kettle or saucepan, put in the pieces of
fish, potatoes, onions and tomatoes, and strain
the poaching liquid over them. Cook 20 minutes
at a gentle simmer, until the potatoes are
tender. Stir in the Vermouth, Sherry, and lemon
juice, cook 2 or 3 minutes longer, remove from
heat, stir in the butter, and serve in soup plates
with hot biscuits or thick-sliced, crusty French
bread. Serves 6 to 8.

## Whitefish

This freshwater relative of the herring and shad is also akin to the trout; indeed, before pollution drastically reduced the whitefish that were once so numerous in Midwestern waters, the fish was often called "white salmon." Other names applied regionally to the whitefish are frostfish, tulibee, highback, humpback, bowback and pilotfish.

Given its family connections, you can readily choose recipes in addition to those that follow for cooking whitefish. And the recipes given for whitefish are also suited for fish unrelated, but with similar physical characteristics, such as the sucker, buffalo, and smelt.

## Whitefish Balls

3-pound fish (approximately)
1 pint fish stock (page 46)
1 pint cold water
1 tablespoon cornstarch
1 tablespoon flour
1½ teaspoons salt
1 egg, lightly beaten
¼ teaspoon freshly-ground white pepper
⅛ teaspoon nutmeg
2 cups milk, very cold, or use evaporated milk diluted with equal parts water

Poach the cleaned fish in a mixture of the stock and cold water. Start cooking with the liquid cold, bring to a boil and skim off froth, then reduce to a simmer, cover the pan, and cook 20 to 25 minutes. Drain the fish, skin, and flake off the flesh. Put the flesh through a meat grinder, using the coarse blade, work into it the cornstarch, flour, and salt, and then pass it through the grinder a second time. Beat the pepper and nutmeg into the egg and work this into the fish; then beat in the milk by spoonsful, using a wooden spoon in a chilled mixing bowl—the best way to do this is to set the mixing bowl in a bed of ice while blending in the milk. Handle the mixture very lightly while forming it into balls about 1 inch in diameter. Poach the balls in the simmering stock in which the fish was cooked, turning them as they poach so they will cook evenly. Cooking time will be 10 to 15 minutes. Drain the fishballs onto cloth or paper towels, and then serve with a warmed white sauce, such as Béchamel (page 166). Serves 4 to 6.

## Whitefish Chowder

3½ to 4-pound fish, cleaned and scaled
1½ quarts cold water
1 bay leaf
8 or 10 peppercorns, cracked or nicked with a knife
2 whole cloves
6 or 8 sprigs fresh parsley
2 or 3 celery tops with leaves
½ cup grated sweet onion
½ cup coarsely-chopped celery
2 cups raw potato diced ½ inch
1½ teaspoons salt
2 cups milk or evaporated milk diluted with equal parts water
1 tablespoon butter or solid margarine

1 tablespoon flour
½ cup heavy cream or undiluted evaporated milk

Put the fish into cold water with the bay leaf, peppercorns, cloves, parsley and celery tops. Bring to a boil, reduce to a simmer, and cook covered for 20 to 25 minutes. Remove the fish, drain, skin, and flake all flesh off bones. Strain the poaching liquid into a clean saucepan, put in the onion, celery, potatoes and salt, and cook briskly until potatoes begin to get tender. Add the fish and milk, and simmer without boiling for 5 minutes. Knead the butter and flour into a smooth paste and flake into the pot, stirring to dissolve it; cook 3 or 4 minutes after the last addition. Remove from heat, stir in the cream, and serve over toasted bread cubes in soup bowls. Serves 6 to 8.

If you still have any doubts that rough fish can be prepared in a number of tasty ways, resolve them in the next chapter, which tells you what to do with plain poached fish or leftovers.

# 11

## MISCELLANEOUS DISHES AND LEFTOVERS

What we have here is a smattering of recipes versatile enough to be adapted to almost any kind of fish that come your way. There are also some suggestions for using the leftover flesh of fish you've cooked by almost any style.

It's not likely that you'd want to sacrifice the delicate flavor of a trout or bass to one of the chowders, but both are especially good in the Belgian fish soup given here. And all fish respond happily to the traditional Matelotes from France.

In the portion of the chapter devoted to leftovers, you'll find ways to deal appetizingly with those embarassing bits and pieces remaining from a fish dinner. Here, the type of fish is of small importance; you can use what's on hand, combine trout with bass or carp with salmon to produce fishcakes, a loaf, or a dish of *pasta*. And the recipes for leftovers are handy guides to the preparation of rough fish as well.

### Waterzoie—Belgian Fish Soup

2 to 3 pounds raw fish
1 quart cold water
1½ teaspoons salt
Large dash cayenne

3 leeks, the green tops discarded, the white portions cut into thin strips

3 tablespoons minced fresh parsley

2 tablespoons butter or solid margarine

Cut the fish into thumb-sized pieces, removing skin and big bones. Put all ingredients except the butter into a deep pot, bring to a boil, and then reduce to a simmer. Cook for 20 minutes, remove from heat, stir in the butter, and ladle into soup bowls. Serves 6 to 8.

## Indo-China Style Fish Chowder

3 pounds fish

1 teaspoon salt

1 pint (approximately) fish stock (page 46)

2 teaspoons lemon or lime juice

1 large sweet onion, sliced thin

3 red-ripe tomatoes, quartered

4 large white radishes, peeled and diced ½ inch

2 sweet green (Bell) peppers, cleaned and cut into thin strips

Juice of 1 lime

Cut the cleaned fish into 1-inch slices, remove skin and backbone, and divide each slice into 2 or 3 pieces. Dust with salt, and let rest for 10 minutes. Combine the stock and lime juice, put in the fish pieces and vegetables, bring to a quick boil, reduce to a simmer, and cook 15 to 20 minutes; the pepper and radishes should be crisp rather than soft. Remove from heat, stir in the juice of 1 lime, and serve on or with boiled rice. Serves 6 to 8.

## Matelote with Red Wine

3 pounds fish, preferably 3 small fish of about 1 pound each
1 tablespoon butter (no substitutes)
12 to 15 small boiling onions, about 1 inch in diameter
½ pound button mushrooms
3 tablespoons brandy—preferably cognac
3 cups dry red Burgundy-type wine (see page 178)
3 cups cold water
*Bouquet garni* in a cheesecloth bag:
    3 sprigs parsley
    2 pieces celery top with leaves
    1 clove garlic cut in half
1 teaspoon salt
2 tablespoons butter (no substitutes)
2 tablespoons flour

Cut the fish across the body into 1-inch slices, discarding fins, tails, heads, and backbone pieces. In a deep saucepan, melt the butter and roll the onions in it over low heat until they begin to turn golden. Add the mushrooms and cook for 2 minutes with gentle stirring. Put in the pieces of fish, warm the brandy, ignite it, and pour over the contents of the pan. When the flames die, pour in the wine and water, add the *bouquet garni,* and salt. Simmer 20 minutes. Remove the *bouquet garni,* drain the fish pieces, onions and mushrooms from the pan and reserve them in a deep, warmed bowl. Knead the butter and flour into a smooth paste and flake it into the sauce while it simmers; stir to dissolve the flakes. Cook for 3 minutes after the last bits dissolve. Pour the sauce over the fish, and serve with thick slices of crusty French bread to be dunked in the sauce between bites. Serves 6.

## Matelote with White Wine

3 pounds fish, preferably 3 small fish of about 1 pound each

1 tablespoon butter (no substitutes)

12 to 15 small white onions about 1 inch in diameter

3 tablespoons brandy—preferably cognac

1½ pints dry, white Burgundy-type wine (see page 178)

2 cups cold water

2 cloves garlic, dropped in boiling water for 1 minute, then drained and mashed

1 teaspoon salt

*Bouquet garni* in a cheesecloth bag:

    2 sprigs fresh parsley

    Large sprig rosemary

    2 whole cloves

    4 or 5 peppercorns, cracked or nicked with a knife

2 hard-cooked eggs, sliced thickly

Thick slices of toasted French bread

Cut the fish into pieces of approximately equal size, about 1-inch chunks. Discard heads, tails, fins, skin, and backbone pieces. Heat the butter in a deep pan, and roll the onions around in it over gentle heat until they begin to show color. Add the pieces of fish, heat the brandy and ignite it; pour over the onions and fish.

When the flames die, add the wine, water, salt, garlic, and the *bouquet garni*. Simmer very gently for 20 minutes. Remove the *bouquet garni* and add the egg slices. Serve in soup plates, spooning the portions over thick slices of crusty French bread in the bottoms of the plates. Serves 6.

## Fishcakes

1 pound—about 2½ cups—cooked flaked fish
1 egg
2 slices firm bread, dry but not hard (Try to find a good solid bread rather than that produced by the mass-production bakeries, which turns into a soggy mess when used in cooking. Small independent bakeries often produce a genuine bread; nationally, Orowheat and Amana offer real breads, including a toasting bread that is ideal for use in cooking.)
1 teaspoon salt
Dash cayenne or Nepal pepper
2 or 3 tablespoons milk or evaporated milk diluted with equal parts water
Fat for sautéing

Combine all ingredients, breaking the bread into small pieces. Your mixture should be just moist enough to hold together, not wet or soggy. Let the mixed ingredients stand in a covered bowl for 40 minutes before forming the cakes. Sauté in hot fat over moderate heat until browned on both sides. Sauce Bercy, page 175, or the Swedish Dill Sauce on page 176, go well with these fishcakes. Makes 10 to 12 cakes about 2½ inches in diameter.

## Baked Fish Loaf

3 cups cooked flaked fish
1 cup coarse dry breadcrumbs or unsalted
  cracker crumbs
¼ cup melted butter or margarine
3 eggs, lightly beaten
1½ tablespoons minced fresh parsley
¼ teaspoon crumbled thyme
¾ teaspoon salt
Large dash freshly-ground white pepper
¼ to ½ cup warm milk, or evaporated milk
  diluted with equal parts water

Combine the ingredients dry and moisten
with the milk; use only enough milk to give the
mixture firmness and smooth texture. Press very
lightly into a buttered loaf pan, put the pan in
a larger pan containing 1 to 1½ inches of water,
and cook in a preheated 375-degree oven for 35
to 40 minutes. Serve hot or cold, choosing a
sauce to match the type of service. Serves 6 to 8.

## Steamed Fish Loaf

3½ to 4 pounds raw fish, cleaned, skinned,
  boned
3 tablespoons beaten butter (no substitutes—
  beaten butter is not "extended" butter, but
  softened butter beaten to soft creaminess
  with a wooden spoon)
½ cup capers
½ teaspoon shredded tarragon leaves

½ teaspoon coarsely-ground pepper
¼ teaspoon nutmeg
1 teaspoon salt
Large piece of cheesecloth or other white cloth
3 cups dry white Burgundy-type wine (see page 178)
1 cup water
1 medium-sized sweet onion, peeled and quartered
4 whole cloves
3 celery tops with leaves
4 sprigs parsley

Shred the flesh of the uncooked fish off the bones; a fork does the job easily. Combine butter, capers and seasonings with the fish meat, using a wooden spoon. Dampen the cloth and spread it out flat, turn the fish mixture onto it, and gently form it into a loaf about 3 inches thick. Bring the cloth over and around the loaf, and tie loosely with heavy string to keep it in place. Bring the wine and water to a simmer in a long, deep pan, add the remaining ingredients, lower the loaf into the pan, cover, and cook for 45 minutes without removing the lid. Lift the loaf out to a warmed platter and let it rest and drain 10 to 15 minutes before removing the cloth. Serve hot, sliced, with Mustard Butter (page 178) or with your choice of sauces from Chapter 12. It is also good when served cold. Serves 6 to 8.

## Fish with Eggs

Combining fish with eggs is such a simple job that no recipes are really necessary, just a few suggestions to start your imagination working. Cooked flaked fish stirred into eggs being scrambled give a heartier-than-usual dish for breakfast, or for a midnight indulgence. A few spoonsful of flaked fish can be combined with almost any of the white sauces given in Chapter 12 to form the filling for pancakes or a folded omelet. Flaked fish highly seasoned with curry powder and cayenne or Nepal pepper, then mixed with either scrambled or minced, hard-boiled eggs results in the famous British buffet breakfast dish of Kedgeree. Finely-chopped or pounded fish flakes can be combined with the yolks of hard-boiled eggs to provide a different kind of filling for stuffed eggs taken picnicking or served as hors d'oeuvres. With these hints as a starter, go on to create your own fish-egg dishes.

## Fish with Pastas

In preparing paste dishes to be served with a fish sauce, it's well to avoid the heavier *pastas* such as macaroni, bombatelli and manicotti. Instead, use the light, fine types like spaghettini and the formed shapes such as farfalle and stelle. If you are fond of the *pastas,* you will learn to cook them correctly, so that they do not come to the table limp and lifeless.

Use ½ pound of paste to serve 4. Cook it in 2 quarts of water with 2 teaspoons of salt added.

Have the water boiling briskly, and put in the paste a little at a time so the water temperature will not be lowered abruptly. Stir as the paste cooks. Test after 8 to 10 minutes; cut a piece of the paste with the spoon, and if a line of white shows at its center, further cooking is required. The moment that white line of raw starch vanishes from the center of the paste, it is done. Immediately pour cold water into the pot to stop cooking, or turn the paste out into a colander and douse it freely with cold water. Before it cools, combine it with the sauce.

### Fish Sauce for *Pasta:*

- 3 tablespoons olive oil or drawn butter (page 32)
- 2 tablespoons chopped green onion tops
- ½ clove garlic, mashed
- 1½ cups fish stock (page 46)
- 2 tablespoons minced fresh parsley
- 2 cups cooked flaked fish

Heat the fat and sauté the onion tops and garlic until the green begins to darken. Add the fish stock and parsley, bring to a simmer, and put in the flaked fish. Cover, remove from heat, and let stand for 2 or 3 minutes. Combine the cooked paste with the sauce and serve at once. Serve grated Parmesan with the dish—or, stir in a tablespoonful when combining the paste with the sauce. Serves 4 generously.

## Roman-Style Fish and Pasta

½ cup butter or solid margarine
1 clove garlic, mashed or minced
1 tablespoon chopped fresh basil
2 tablespoons chopped fresh parsley
½ cup chopped fresh mushrooms
2 cups flaked cooked fish
½ pound (raw weight) pasta, cooked according to method given on page 161

In a deep saucepan, melt the butter and in it sauté the herbs and mushrooms until the mushrooms are tender. Use low heat, and cook slowly. Add the fish flakes to the pan just long enough to warm them; have the *pasta* cooked and drained, and still hot. Empty the paste over the fish-mushroom mixture in the pan, stir together, and serve. Serves 4.

There are, of course, some kinds of fish that need no dressing-up to make them welcome the second time around. Tender, pink flakes of poached trout or salmon come to mind; all that's required to enhance their flavor is a crisp cracker spread with a tart Mayonnaise or one of the subtle Herbed Butters you will find in the next chapter. And, you can now cook a big fish with the certainty that you'll be using part of it for another meal. You'll cook that monster with confidence, knowing that you have the means to convert what's left into a fresh and tasty dish.

# 12

## SAUCES AND WINES

There is an aphorism associated with classical French cuisine: *"La sauce fait le poisson."* In quick translation, it can be rendered as: "The sauce makes the fish." The phrase is only partly true, of course; there must be freshness and flavor within the fish itself before even the most masterful creator of sauces can produce from it a superb dish. But don't underestimate the contribution made by a good sauce.

For many years, American cooks were shy about saucing, a hesitancy based on misapprehension. It was believed that preparing a sauce is a long, tedious chore, requiring vast knowledge of ingredients and great concentration, to say nothing of talent and long hours of stirring. And, there was a lack of knowledge of the important part played by two or three basic sauces in preparing the minor sauces; with one basic white sauce for stock, three or four other white sauces can be made in minutes.

Then, just when home cooks were losing their sauce shyness, a flood of chemical concoctions from the food factories began crowding the supermarket shelves. They were labelled "instant" and looked enticing, so home cooks tried them; and after tasting them they cannot be blamed for saying to themselves, "If that's what sauces are like, I'll get along without them!"

It's only necessary to read the labels of these products; the tiny print reveals that few contain any natural ingredients, just laboratory chemicals designed to imitate the flavor of a genuine sauce. Some merely taste unfortunate, others are downright nasty. Leave them to the fate they deserve, gathering dust on the shelf, while you prepare good sauces for your fish.

In the sauce section of this chapter, you will find only the lighter white sauces suitable for fish, plus a few spicy ones for the more unruly of the fish family. There are also the classic egg sauces, the real Sauce Tartare, and some suggestions for simple Herbed Butters that let the true flavor of fish come through.

## White Sauces

Before the thought of sauces makes you push the panic button, look at all seven of the traditional white sauces in this section. You will see that two basic sauces provide the foundation for all seven. If you keep on hand in the refrigerator jars of the two basic sauces, you are equipped to make any of their variants in a matter of three or four minutes.

There is only one tricky job in making a white sauce—the preparation of the flour paste, or *roux*, which must be cooked so that all the starch in the flour is converted and no trace of the taste of flour remains. This must be done without letting the flour get brown, a simple matter of watching your cooking temperatures. Basically, all that is ever involved in saucing is keeping an eye on the temperature and having the desire to offer a superior dish.

## Sauce Béchamel

4 tablespoons butter (no substitutes)
½ cup grated onion
4 tablespoons flour
3 pints milk or evaporated milk diluted with equal parts water
3 white peppercorns, cracked or nicked with a knife
½ teaspoon salt
Large pinch nutmeg, preferably freshly-ground
2 sprigs fresh parsley

Melt butter over low heat and sauté the onion until soft, without letting it get brown. Stir in the flour, and cook 3 to 4 minutes. Scald the milk by heating it and removing from heat the moment bubbles begin to appear at the sides of the saucepan. Add the milk to the floured onions by cupsful, stirring briskly as it is poured in. Put in the peppercorns, salt, nutmeg and parsley, and cook without boiling until the liquid is reduced in volume by one-third. Strain into a sterilized jar with a well-fitting lid. The sauce will keep under refrigeration in a closed container for about a month. When being heated for use after refrigeration, it should be thinned with a spoonful or two of milk and heated slowly. Makes about 1 quart sauce.

## Cream Sauce

1 pint Béchamel
½ cup heavy cream or undiluted evaporated milk

Heat the Béchamel without boiling until it is reduced in volume by one-fourth. Stir in the cream, which should be warm but not hot. Generally, when it is to be used on fish, a half teaspoon of lemon juice is added as well. Makes 1¼ cups sauce.

## Sauce Mornay

1 pint Sauce Béchamel
3 egg yolks
1 tablespoon cream or undiluted evaporated milk
3 tablespoons grated Parmesan
2 tablespoons butter (no substitutes)

Warm the Béchamel; do not let it boil. Beat the egg yolks into the cream and stir into the Béchamel, add the cheese, and let cook for 5 minutes. Remove from heat, and stir in the butter to smooth the texture. Makes about 2½ cups sauce.

## Sauce Aurore

1 pint Sauce Mornay
3 tablespoons tomato purée
1 tablespoon butter (no substitutes)

Over low heat, combine the Sauce Mornay and the tomato purée. Heat without boiling 3 or 4 minutes, remove from heat, and stir in the butter to refine the texture of the sauce. Makes about 2⅓ cups sauce.

## Sauce Velouté

4 tablespoons butter or solid margarine (see note at beginning of directions)

4 tablespoons flour

3 pints fish stock (page 46)

3 white peppercorns, cracked or nicked with a knife

1 teaspoon salt

½ cup mushroom bits and pieces, preferably stems and shavings from fresh mushrooms

(It is practical to substitute margarine in this sauce, since neither the Velouté nor the minor sauces based upon it use acid ingredients. However, since none of the white sauces uses a great quantity of butter, its use is recommended in their preparation.)

Melt butter over low heat and stir in the flour to make a smooth paste. Do not allow the flour to brown, and cook long enough—about 3 or 4 minutes—after adding the last of the flour to make sure all its starch is converted; this avoids an unpleasant starchy taste in the finished sauce. Have the fish stock boiling, and when the butter-flour roux is ready, add the boiling stock a third at a time, stirring briskly. Put in the peppercorns, salt and mushrooms, and simmer without boiling until the liquid is reduced in volume by one-fourth. Stir occasionally to prevent it from sticking to the pan; even if you're using a Teflon-lined pan, it will stick unless stirred now and then. Strain through a cloth into a sterilized jar having a tight-fitting cover. The sauce will keep for about a month under refrigeration in a closed container. When using the Velouté after it has been stored, add a spoonful or two of warm stock or water and heat gently, without boiling. Makes about 1⅓ pints of sauce.

## Sauce Suprême

1 pint fish stock (page 46)
½ cup bits and pieces of fresh mushrooms
1 cup Sauce Velouté
1 cup cream or undiluted evaporated milk
Large dash cayenne
1 tablespoon butter or solid margarine

Boil the fish stock and the mushroom bits together until the stock is reduced in volume by two-thirds. Remove from heat until boiling stops, stir in the Velouté, and simmer without boiling until it is reduced to half its volume. Add the cream by pouring slowly, while stirring briskly. Remove from heat, and stir in the cayenne and butter. Strain into a sauce boat. Makes about 1 pint sauce.

## Sauce Allemande

1 pint Sauce Suprême
2 egg yolks
1 tablespoon cream or undiluted evaporated milk

Heat the Sauce Suprême gently, without boiling. Beat the egg yolks with the cream and stir into the sauce. Bring to the scalding point (when bubbles appear at the edges of the pan), but do not allow to boil. Remove from heat at once and strain into a sauce boat or over the dish to be sauced. Makes about 1⅓ pints sauce.

## Egg Sauces

Most cooks have a fear of trying to prepare the very simple egg sauces, Hollandaise and Mayonnaise. They've never attempted them, you understand, but they've heard or read how hard they are to make.

In actual fact, both are very easy, whether composed by hand or with the aid of an electric blender. For hand preparation there is one tool that can correctly be called indispensible; it is the wire chef's whisk, properly called a *fouet,* which is the sauce maker's best friend and the best device yet created for blending eggs and fats into a smooth emulsion. If you cannot find these whisks in your local stores, Bon Apetit, 113 South 19th St., Philadelphia, Pa. 19103, has an unusually complete selection: the 8-inch size, most useful in sauce making, is 35 cents, the 10-inch size, 50 cents, and they will supply you by mail. And if you own a blender, you can produce egg sauces to your heart's content without lifting a finger except to press a button.

Based on Hollandaise and Mayonnaise are other sauces useful in giving verve to fish dishes: Sauce Verte, Sauce Mousseline, and Sauce Tartare. The latter, by the way, is much more than the blob of pickle-studded mayonnaise served under the name, yet is easier to prepare than a dish of boiled water.

# Sauce Hollandaise (traditional method)

3 egg yolks
1 tablespoon warm water
½ pound butter (no substitutes)
¼ teaspoon salt
Generous dash of cayenne
2 tablespoons fresh lemon juice

In the top of a double boiler, over simmering water, beat the egg yolks with 1 tablespoon hot water until they are creamy. Add the butter in small dollops, beating constantly, and incorporating each piece before putting in another. When all the butter is added, beat in the cayenne and lemon juice. Hollandaise prepared by the traditional method tends to separate when stored in the refrigerator; it is easily reconstituted by heating gently and whisking in about ½ tablespoon of warm water. Makes about 1 cup sauce.

# Sauce Hollandaise (blender method)

½ cup butter (no substitutes)
3 egg yolks
2 tablespoons fresh lemon juice
¼ teaspoon salt
Large dash of cayenne

Heat the butter until it begins to bubble. Have the other ingredients in the blender, waiting. Start the blender on LOW speed, remove the cover at once, and pour in the melted butter. Turn off the blender when all the butter has been added. Pour the sauce at once into a metal container and put this container into a larger one containing hot but not boiling water. (This final step is very important. If it is not done, your sauce will be thin and runny instead of smooth and creamy.) Leave the sauce in the hot water for at least 5 minutes; it can stay longer without any harm being done. Hollandaise prepared in the blender will not separate under refrigeration; it can be made ready to serve by putting its container into a pan of almost-boiling water until the sauce thins enough to pour readily. Makes about ¾ cup sauce.

## Mayonnaise (traditional method)

3 egg yolks
1 tablespoon fresh lemon juice
¼ teaspoon prepared Dijon-type mustard
Generous pinch salt
Large dash freshly-ground white pepper
Pinch of cayenne or Nepal pepper
2½ cups olive oil or peanut oil

Beat the egg yolks with the lemon juice, adding the seasonings, until the eggs are very creamy. Begin adding the oil a little at a time, approximately by teaspoonsful, beating well between each addition. Beat until all the oil has been added and the sauce is a little thicker than you think it should be. Then beat in 1 tablespoon of very hot water; this will keep the Mayonnaise from separating when stored in the refrigerator. Makes about 1¾ cups Mayonnaise.

## Mayonnaise (blender method)

1 egg
½ teaspoon sugar
¾ teaspoon salt
½ teaspoon prepared Dijon-type mustard
Very generous pinch of cayenne or Nepal
    pepper
3 tablespoons fresh lemon juice or 1½ table-
    spoons each lemon juice and vinegar, for
    a very sharp Mayonnaise
1 cup olive oil or peanut oil

Put the egg, all seasonings, the lemon juice, and ⅓ of the oil in the blender. Turn on LOW speed, take off the cover and pour in the rest of the oil quite rapidly. Replace cover, turn blender switch to HIGH and run for 10 to 15 seconds. This Mayonnaise will not separate in the refrigerator. Makes about 1 pint.

## Sauce Mousseline

1 pint Mayonnaise or Hollandaise
½ cup whipped cream

Fold the whipped cream into the Mayonnaise or Hollandaise, whichever you choose as the base for your Mousseline. (There is another Sauce Mousseline, made by folding 2 egg whites, beaten stiffly with 1 tablespoon lemon juice, into 1 pint Sauce Velouté. Take your choice.) Makes 1½ pints sauce.

## Sauce Verte

½ pound spinach leaves
1 teaspoon chopped tarragon leaves
1 teaspoon chopped chives
1 teaspoon chopped chervil
1 teaspoon chopped green onion tops
1½ cups Mayonnaise

Wash the spinach and shake it well; do not wipe or blot it dry. Put the spinach and all the herbs into a saucepan and cook covered for 10 minutes over gentle heat. Spread a cloth over a mixing bowl and empty the saucepan onto the cloth; when cool enough to handle, compress the greens by twisting them into a pocket in the cloth, letting the juices strain into the bowl. Combine ½ cup of this juice with the Mayonnaise, beating until smooth. Makes about 2 cups sauce.

## Sauce Tartare

2 hard-boiled egg yolks
½ teaspoon salt
⅛ teaspoon freshly-ground white pepper
1 cup olive or peanut oil
1 teaspoon tarragon vinegar
½ teaspoon minced chives, or minced tops of young green onions
½ cup Mayonnaise

Pound the egg yolks into a smooth paste, incorporating the salt, pepper and oil into it while pounding. Beat the vinegar into the egg-yolk paste with a whisk; then blend this with the minced herbs and Mayonnaise. Makes about ¾ cup sauce.

## Quick Sauces

Any one of the trio of traditional sauces that follow can be prepared in a very short time. Two of the sauces, Sauce Bercy and the New Orleans Fish Sauce, are best when served warm. The Swedish Dill Sauce is one that should not be heated.

## Sauce Bercy

1 tablespoon butter (no substitutes)
1 teaspoon minced shallots
½ cup dry white Burgundy-type wine (see page 178)
1¼ cups fish stock (page 46)
1 tablespoon butter (no substitutes)
1 tablespoon flour
½ teaspoon salt
1 teaspoon minced fresh parsley

Melt butter over gentle heat and sauté the shallots until they are soft without allowing them to brown. Add the wine, and cook for 10 minutes at a soft simmer; crush the shallots with the stirring spoon and blend them into the liquid. Blend butter and flour into a smooth paste and flake it into the liquid, stirring as it dissolves. Cook 3 to 4 minutes after the last flake of flour disappears; then add the salt and parsley. Cook for 5 minutes, stirring occasionally, and pour the sauce into a sauce boat or over the dish to be sauced. Makes about 2 cups sauce.

## Swedish Dill Sauce

½ cup cider or malt vinegar
1½ cups olive oil or peanut oil
1 teaspoon lemon juice
Large dash cayenne
4 drops Tabasco Sauce
Tiny pinch of dry mustard
2 tablespoons chopped fresh dill, or 3 tablespoons crushed dillseed
3 tablespoons whipped cream

Using an electric beater at high speed or a blender at low speed, combine all ingredients except the whipped cream. (The combining can be done by hand, if you have neither of these appliances. Use a wire whisk to beat the vinegar and oil into a smooth emulsion, pound the seasonings and dill with the lemon juice to form a light paste and beat it into the oil-vinegar mixture.) When all ingredients are blended, fold the whipped cream in with a whisk or spatula. This sauce is usually chilled very lightly and served with broiled or fried fish. Makes about 2½ cups sauce.

## New Orleans Fish Sauce

1 cup chopped sweet onion
3 celery tops with leaves, chopped
½ teaspoon salt
¼ teaspoon freshly-ground pepper
1 teaspoon minced chervil
1 tablespoon minced fresh parsley
2½ cups fish stock (page 46)
2 tablespoons flour

1 **tablespoon butter or solid margarine**
2 **egg yolks**
3 **drops Tabasco Sauce**

In a saucepan, simmer the onion, celery, seasonings and herbs in the fish stock. Cook for 15 minutes, over medium heat. Knead the flour and butter into a smooth paste, beat the egg yolks lightly, and cream the two together with a wooden spoon until light and fluffy. Strain the liquid from the saucepan into a clean pan, and over low heat add the creamed flour-egg yolk mixture by spoonsful, stirring until it dissolves and a smooth sauce results. Remove from heat and add the Tabasco. The sauce is usually served hot or warm. Makes about 2½ cups sauce.

## Herbed Butters

These are very useful as quick, simple seasonings for fish that are simply sautéed or poached. Their range is limited only by your own imagination. Any herb or spice can be blended with butter to make a quick and easy sauce. When substituting margarine for butter, remember that even some solid margarines today contain the foam-retardant chemicals that also keep the butter from blending with acids such as lemon juice and vinegars. Substitute if you wish, but test before you embark upon the preparation of a large quantity.

*Anchovy Butter:* ½ drained anchovy fillet or a pea-sized pellet of anchovy paste blended with 1 tablespoon butter.

*Colbert Butter:* ¼ teaspoon meat extract (BV, Bovril, etc.) and a pinch of minced tarragon to 1 tablespoon butter.

*Maitre d'Hotel Butter:* a pinch of chopped parsley, a dash of lemon juice, a touch of freshly-ground white pepper to 1 tablespoon butter.

*Mustard Butter:* ⅛ teaspoon prepared Dijon-type mustard to 1 tablespoon butter.

*Shrimp Butter:* 1 tablespoon cooked shrimp pounded to a smooth paste and blended with 1 tablespoon butter. (These proportions apply to any compound butter made from shellfish or fish.)

All of these are prepared simply by kneading the ingredients together; to prepare larger quantities, simply double or triple the indicated amounts. Use them hot or cold.

## Wines

Whether to be used in cooking or drunk at the table, wine selection becomes a matter of personal taste. This section is written for the novice, approaching wine for the first time. If your tastes are already formed, your opinions set, your likes and dislikes established, or if you have a cellar stacked with bottles of impeccable vintage awaiting your pleasure, stop reading right here.

On the other hand, if you're bewildered by the word "Burgundy" and rattled by the word "Rhine," if you gaze in honest uncertainty at the scores of labels on hundreds of bottles staring at you from a dealer's shelves, this part of the book is for you. It won't make you an expert. A couple of pages in a book devoted primarily to fish recipes is no substitute for years of tasting and exploring the nuances of flavors in the bottles to which all those labels are pasted.

To begin, let's divide wines into their respective groups. There are three: still, fortified, and sparkling. The first group is often called table wine; these are the kind you use in most recipes and the kind you drink with dinner. The second group includes some wines often encountered in cooking; as beverages, they are usually offered before or after a meal, and are frequently referred to as cocktail or dessert wines. The third group is made up of wines only infrequently called for in recipes, and generally reserved for drinking on special occasions.

Now, in highly-condensed form, here are the taste characteristics of the most commonly-used wines:

Red Burgundy is robust, vigorous, full-bodied and very dry. White Burgundy is as full-bodied as the red and usually of a flinty tartness. The lesser red Burgundy, Beaujolais, is a dryly-soft, fruity wine that has no precise U.S. counterpart.

Bordeaux, or Claret, has a long and pleasantly astringent taste, somewhat flat in the young red Bordeaux wines most commonly available. White Bordeaux has a tremendous range of flavors, from very dry and almost heavy to a delicate shimmering dryness that nearly approaches sweetness.

Rhine wines, invariably white, are light and fruity with a basic sweetness. Moselles, also white, are somewhat thinner of body and a trifle more astringency shows through their sweetness.

Chianti is dry, hearty and rich. It has no U.S. counterpart, just as U.S. Zinfandel has none in Europe. Zinfandel's flavor straddles a line between the fruitiness of Beaujolais and the flatness of Claret.

Rosé wines are rarely used in cooking; although they are pleasant to drink, heat kills their light flavor. Rosés are the least compatible of all wines with fish dishes.

Champagne, in the sparkling wines, has limited use in cooking; its chief charm is its effervescence, which is lost in the sauce pot. Sparkling Burgundy is in the same class with rosé: useless in cooking, and incompatible with fish dishes.

Sherry, among the fortified wines, is the most often encountered by the cook. In flavor, Sherry ranges from astringently tart to very sweet—the gradations designated on Spanish labels as Fino, Manzanilla, Amontillado, Amorosa and Olorosa. U.S. vineyards offer a Cocktail Sherry corresponding to Amontillado and a Cream Sherry very close in sweetness to Olorosa.

Madiera and Marsala are the two other fortified wines used in cooking, chiefly in sauces. Port and Angelica are rarely called for in recipes. The U.S. fortified wine called Muscatel is best ignored, being fit neither for cooking nor drinking. U.S. White Port is similarly unattractive.

Liquors are used for flavor in fish cookery chiefly by being ignited in a dish at some stage of its preparation. Recipes will usually specify

Cognac, a rich fruity brandy produced in a limited region of France. Other brandies can be used, of course, but lack the grapiness that gives Cognac its distinction.

A quick guide to wine selection, if you find labels confusing, is bottle shapes. Both red and white Burgundies are contained in green slope-shouldered bottles. Bordeaux wines come in bottles with straight sides and pronounced shoulders, red Bordeaux in green glass, white in clear glass. Rhine wines are bottled in tall, slender, brown glass flutes and Moselles in flutes of the same shape, but of green glass.

Another quick guide, this one to the quality of the wine in bottles of any shape, is to look at its closure. Most of the inferior wines produced in Europe or the U.S. are put in bottles with screw-top caps. Vintners who produce the better wines use corks, since the interaction of cork with wine has a definite effect on the aging qualities of the wine. The guide is not infallible and does not apply to rosés, which are not designed to age in the bottle, but it's still a quick and easy method of arriving at a snap decision.

Bottle shapes give you the same at-a-glance clues to domestic wine varieties as they do to those from abroad, the same shaped bottles being identified with the same types of wines as listed above. In the case of varietal wines, U.S. labels are as confusing as European ones, unless you take the time to learn the names of grape varieties. Thus, Pinot Noir corresponds to red Burgundy, and Pinot Blanc or Pinot Chardonnay to white Burgundy; Cabernet or Cabernet Sauvignon equals red Bordeaux, and Semillon and Sauvignon Blanc means white

Bordeaux; Johannisberg Reisling or Sylvaner corresponds to Rhine; Traminer or Gewürztraminer to Moselle. If you're really interested, these are not too many names to remember.

Varietal labels on U.S. wines are important guides to quality, but it's well to remember that many vintners in this country still use the generic European names: Burgundy, Chablis, Claret, Sauterne. The only way you can learn the quality of wine in the bottles labelled this way is to buy and try.

Domestic producers of outstanding wines who distribute nationally are, alphabetically: Almadén, Beaulieu, Beringer, Korbel, Taylor, and Wente. All but Taylor are California-based. There are other fine vintners on both coasts who put out wines in quantities so limited that national distribution is precluded, and it is well worth your while to seek them out.

It goes without saying that absolute uniformity is impossible when cooking with wines. The Burgundy of one vineyard differs from the next, just as substituting Bordeaux for Burgundy in a recipe gives a different flavor to the finished dish. This is of relatively small importance, provided you use common sense in making substitutions. Only a madman would insert a sweet Rhine-type wine into a recipe having herbs and spices balanced to accommodate a hearty white Burgundy. As long as the basic character of a dish is preserved, substitution harms neither the dish nor the one who eats it. One of the most often overlooked aspects of cooking from recipes is that the person preparing a dish cooks it to please himself and his guests, not the chef who composed the recipe.

But do keep one thing in mind: certain traditional recipes specifying a definite type of wine in their ingredients have withstood the test of time, and can generally be counted on to be universally pleasing. A considerate chef-host will remember that those sharing the dishes he prepares may be accustomed to following tradition, in recipes and wine service, and the tastes of the host should always take second place to those of his guests.

# INDEX